A Traveller on Horseback

A Traveller on Horseback

in Eastern Turkey and Iran

Christina Dodwell

Walker and Company
New York

First published in the United States of America in 1989
by Walker Publishing Company, Inc.

First published in the United Kingdom in 1987
by Hodder & Stoughton

Library of Congress Cataloging-in-Publication Data

Dodwell, Christina, 1951–
A traveller on horseback : in eastern Turkey and Iran / Christina Dodwell.
p.   cm.
ISBN 0-8027-1078-6
1. Turkey, Eastern—Description and travel.   2. Iran—Description and
travel—1979–   3. Dodwell, Christina, 1951–   —Journeys—Turkey,
Eastern.   4. Dodwell, Christina, 1951–   —Journeys—Iran.
I. Title.   II. Title: Traveler on horseback.
DS51.E27D63   1989
915.5′0454—dc19   88-33058
                                                                                  CIP

Printed in the United States of America

10   9   8   7   6   5   4   3   2   1

To all the people who helped make my journey such a wonderful experience: very special thanks to Louise and Narcy Firouz in Iran and to Sema Yaman in Turkey, and for those not in the book but whom I wish to thank:

In London: Archdeacon and Mrs Peter Mallett, Zia Beyandor, Vivienne Sharp, Kabir Ahmed and Roshan and David Reddaway.

In Turkey: Gordon and Gael Graham, and Mike Windus in Izmir; the Alemdag family in Istanbul; the Yaman family of Adana; Ataman Yemisciaglu in Erzurum and Anthony Fitzherbert of FAO.

In Pakistan: Horst and Gudrun Wischmeyer (Quetta), and General Sardar and Soraiya Lodi (Karachi).

What really made me love both Iran and Turkey was the spontaneous kindness of people I met, and my final thanks go to the village muhtars and the people of the land.

Contents

Illustrations

One

CAPPADOCIA

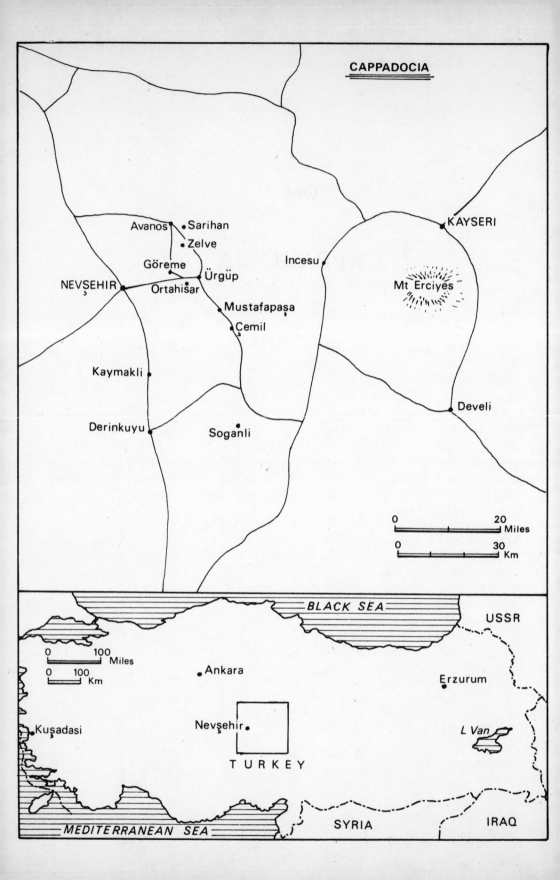

CAPPADOCIA

Sarihan

Avanos

Zelve

Göreme

KAYSERI

Ürgüp

Incesu

NEVŞEHIR

Ortahisar

Mt Erciyes

Mustafapaşa

Cemil

Kaymakli

Develi

Derinkuyu

Soganli

0   20
Miles

0   30
Km

BLACK SEA

USSR

Ankara

Erzurum

Nevşehir

0   100
Miles

L Van

0   100
Km

Kuşadasi

T U R K E Y

MEDITERRANEAN SEA

SYRIA

IRAQ

1 *Cappadocia gesiorum*

It was time for me to go travelling again by horse. I knew the journey would be more fun in a wild part of the world, and what particularly attracted me were the remoter regions of Turkey and Iran.

It's odd how people try to put a woman off such ideas by saying it's too dangerous and she might be killed. My instinct told me that this was unlikely; in all the other journeys I've made the same warnings have been untrue. As for the threat of bandits or arrest by revolutionaries, I trusted in my common sense and doubted there would still be bandits nowadays.

Turkey's strategic position as a land-bridge spanning two continents has given it a colourful ten thousand years of surging and receding invasions. But it was surprisingly difficult to buy a good map. The Turkish ones had enlargements of western Turkey but the east was shown only in small scale and much of it looked empty. The lack of main roads would be no problem on horseback, however.

My departure, early in May, coincided with the Greek Orthodox Church's Easter celebrations in Athens which, being en route, I couldn't resist. And a short stop in Greece would give me the chance to look into my great-many-times-great-uncle Edward Dodwell's journey by mule across Greece in the early nineteenth century. He had been travelling to find and record ruins of historical and religious interest.

The festivities for Greek Easter culminated on the day I arrived and that night I followed a brass band, along streets lined with soldiers standing at attention, to Athens' main cathedral. Other regiments converged, marching with equal pomp; one group in white blousy tunics and tight leggings marched by sliding their feet along the ground in an unusual shuffle. Leaving the parades, I slipped up back alleys heading for the hilltop at Likavetos where a different sort of festival would take place.

The alleys were dimly lit and I had to dodge as someone

threw a bucket of water from an upstairs balcony. Many people were heading for Likavetos, soon we were a throng. On top of the peak the terraces round the chapel of St George were so crowded that walking was impossible. I wriggled slowly through the mass. Inside the church a priest intoned litanies and a crown of thorns was prominently displayed. A man sold me a candle. Everyone was holding candles, some ornate with ribbons and lace. They would all light their candles from the sacred flame on the altar at midnight.

The packed church was hot and stuffy so I retreated outside and found a space to sit on the wall overlooking Athens, a denseness of city lights encircled by darkness, making it an island surrounded by the night. We were high above the Acropolis' illuminated shape. The city sky below us jumped with firecrackers and flashed with fireworks, the displays growing more spectacular each minute.

At midnight on the hill the priests brought out their finest jewelled crosses and announced, 'Christ has risen from the dead.' The church bells started pealing, rockets flooded the sky, the crowd began to sing. The sacred flame was passed from candle to candle, each person lighting from another, a small boy lit mine, and slowly everyone formed a procession leading down the winding hillside path. I watched from the summit as the procession grew. People walked carefully shielding their candles, trying to reach home with them still alight. Then they make the sign of the cross with the flame on the door and it's said to bring good luck all the year. My candle burned steadily and my fingers got glued together with hot wax. In some way my journey began with that procession down the hillside.

I spent nearly a week in Greece, crossing my old Uncle Edward's route on Peloponnese hillsides ablaze with scarlet poppies. It felt marvellous to be out under a warm sun after England's long cold winter. Edward Dodwell had felt a sense of liberation even greater than mine, for he was a prisoner on parole, having been captured in France in the Napoleonic Wars. As a parole prisoner, he was not allowed to return to Britain, so he went travelling instead. The temples and fortresses that he and I visited are now too well-known to need description here, though their columns and walls gave me a sense of infinity which I enjoyed. But, despite the temptation to continue through Greece, I decided not to be side-tracked from Turkey and Iran.

So I caught a ferry-yacht across the Aegean, pottering between islands along rugged coastlines, and disembarked at the small Turkish port of Kuşadasi. After immigration formalities, I bought a ticket for the next day's bus to Nevşehir which is about 700 kilometres east on the central Anatolian Plateau and halfway across Turkey. Then I found a campsite where I slung my hammock.

The bus was efficient, cheap and fast. We were offered sprinklings of cologne on our hands; the other passengers all rubbed their hands together, then over their faces, sniffing a whiff up their noses, before finally smoothing their hair with their hands. It seems that men are not allowed to sit next to an unrelated woman, so someone's mother sat by me, whether for my moral protection or the men's, I wondered. She was fat and homely, easy for me to relax with, though she was slightly shocked to discover I have no husband and children. She clicked with disapproval, and suggested I'd be wise to tell Turkish men that my husband and children were awaiting me at my destination. The bus stopped for a break while passengers had a meal, and several times for tea. During one stop my companion ordered coffee for us. This was special treatment for, contrary to what you might expect, Turks drink more tea than coffee since nowadays coffee is expensive. Afterwards she told my fortune from the upturned coffee grains. Her rural accent was so strong I could only understand that both accidents and joys were in store.

By dawn we had climbed on to the Anatolian Plateau and it was cold. The bus terminated in Nevşehir and I caught a *dolmuş*, the useful Turkish cross between a taxi and a minibus, to Ürgüp, a village in the heart of Cappadocia's most exciting and beautiful region. Mount Erciyes loomed ahead, an extinct volcano 4,300 metres high and permanently covered in snow. Wonderful scenery opened up all around, I wished we were going more slowly and resolved to look for a horse in Ürgüp's local bazaar, so that I could see the region in my own way.

Ürgüp is a small town of cobbled streets and old stone houses nestling against a hill honeycombed with semi-troglodyte dwellings. Walking through the bazaar, I enjoyed the colours of the fruit and vegetables. The women selling them wore yashmaks and the men woolly hats; one man told me what the fruits on his stall are called in Turkish. He pointed at some unripe plums and said, 'My name is Eric.'

The rest of the bazaar was selling *salvar* (baggy trousers), knives, pottery and cloth. The livestock section was a short walk away, it had a few bunches of cattle and sheep, and three good-sized ponies.

The first one I looked at was obviously unsuitable, it had a swollen fetlock; in fact none of them was a beauty, they were scraggy and unkempt. Only one had any potential, he was an even-tempered white stallion and, although he had no saddle, he was well behaved when I rode him at the back of the livestock area. A look at his teeth told me he was no youngster, which actually didn't matter since an older pony is often a more sensible and experienced travelling companion.

My previous horses have come from slaughter yards or been rejects no one could ride, so it wasn't his quality that worried me. Yet I wasn't very enthusiastic about buying him. The owner saw my reluctance and suggested, very kindly, that I hire the pony from him for a few days, and decide later whether or not to buy it. He also agreed to lend me a saddle and bridle, and to stable the pony on the nights I returned to Ürgüp. It seemed as good an arrangement as any and I was eager to begin exploring. So early the next morning I collected the pony, named Beyaz (which means white), and set off uphill out of sleepy Ürgüp.

The fast of Ramadan, or Ramazan as it's called by non-Arab Moslems, had begun today and people were in no hurry to start a long hungry day, forbidden by Islamic law to eat or drink until after sunset. The empty cobbled streets rang beneath Beyaz' hooves. We had a steep climb for two kilometres, then cut across country on the borders of vine plantations and fields of yellow-flowering rapeseed, and emerged on a crag overlooking a surrealistic volcanic landscape where valleys of soft pink, honey and pale green rock had been eroded into tall tapering shapes. There were hundreds of small conical hills, and groups of multi-spired formations.

Beyaz was blown by the climb so I gave him a ten-minute break while I repacked the saddlebags to balance their weight. The bags are a pair I made from a tent's flysheet, they hang over the back of the saddle and I put an extra cinch to prevent them flapping around when cantering, which could alarm a horse.

We reached a mineral spring which is said locally to cure eczema and stomach ailments. Two young women were filling buckets and I splashed water on my face to try and alleviate an attack of hayfever sneezing – I get hayfever because I am allergic to horses – and, when I sneezed, one of the women said, 'Çok yaşa,' which her friend translated for me as, 'I wish you many years not dead.'

From there I rode to the small town of Ortahisar, set in a valley. The town is dominated by a castle constructed within a tall plug of sheer-sided rock; tunnels and caverns are the passages and chambers. I rode on, eager to reach the fabled rock-hewn churches of Göreme; there are reported to be over three hundred churches in one valley.

As we approached Göreme valley I looked for a back entrance and found a path along a damp narrow ravine which in places was scarcely wide enough for a horse and saddlebags. Looking up above the ravine I began to notice the backs of partially fallen rock churches and some of their walls decorated with simple red line drawings that date back to AD 300, the first local attempts at cave painting. Later paintings were in green and red lines, and by the Byzantine era the art had been long established.

Tethering Beyaz in some lush grass, I scrambled up the ravine's side and explored other outlying churches. They had been made by hollowing out the interior of rock-cones. This type of volcanic rock is tufa, beloved of Western garden centres. It is so soft that it can easily be carved out by primitive tools. When air comes in contact with the rock, its surface hardens; a useful building material.

The earliest dwellings were hewn out around 4000 BC, though the majority here now date back to AD 300; it was only later in the Byzantine era that they were turned into churches. The glory of the churches was their frescoes. One nearby chapel's cavernous interior was coated with pictures of the Crucifixion and Resurrection painted in the style of a strip cartoon with dividing boxes drawn around each episode.

When Beyaz and I arrived at the main entrance to Göreme's open air museum, the gatekeeper said that horses were not allowed in, I must park him in the car park. It was a small car park with coaches trying to manoeuvre into spaces, not a good place for a horse, but nearby was a grassy dell and a convenient signpost for a tether. Predictably the sign read 'No Parking'.

Inside a hillock I found a nun's convent where a ten-metre-long refectory table has been chiselled in the rock with a carved rock bench all around it. Convenient niches once held kitchen pots and cooking fires. Most of the churches have grave-holes dug in the floor, many of them child-size, and I realised that each church had belonged to a different family who buried their dead in their own sacred place.

I was puzzled by a series of square niches hewn high up in a cliff face, until I noticed pigeons flying in and out – ancient pigeon lofts.

After collecting Beyaz I rode west along a track up another valley. The track vanished into a stream bed which was fortunately only a rivulet on a firm sandy base. We progressed for several kilometres before the stream bed grew smaller and the valley narrowed. Its pale pink rocks bulged into our path but, each time I thought we were blocked, the way opened up a little, with space on the stream banks for cultivation of crops and fruit trees.

Hewn in the canyon sides were special caves for the storage of fruit, which keeps throughout the year without going bad. The early inhabitants had discovered this, and they also made caves for storing wheat, which lasts best in low-oxygen conditions. Their wheat storage was particularly ingenious because mice cannot get into sealed caves; weevils can't survive if there's too much carbon dioxide; and since wheat naturally produces its own level of carbon dioxide, it creates its own low-oxygen environment. Western farmers have now developed this system and they call it the silo.

A cart came along carrying a man who had been taken severely ill; I suspected he was in for a long ride to reach a hospital. At noon we rested in verdant shade and after I had unsaddled Beyaz he rolled and rolled with pleasure in the lush grass. While I picnicked and rambled among the rocks, Beyaz made no attempt to stray or run off.

The valley ended for us when the path was barred by rocks, so we turned back, splashing along the sandy stream in a low bounding canter. What a comfortable easy-going steed he was.

Another valley we explored had a series of needle rocks resembling tall candles, complete with flame; the flame being a darker harder core that has eroded coarsely tapering. I gave Beyaz a half-hour rest there, but afterwards didn't tighten the saddle girth properly and on an uphill scramble the saddle and saddlebags slipped. Beyaz leapt forward, making matters worse; the saddle slid out sideways underneath me and I realised I was about to be thrown.

Pushing hard on the stirrup which was rising I made a last desperate bid to right things, but Beyaz was plunging on the steep slope and I was tossed into the air. Not a fall, I landed on my feet beside the startled Beyaz. With the saddle and bags now hanging upsidedown under his belly, he threatened to panic, and I clung to his reins while he dashed in tight circles around me. Things went flying out of the saddlebags; pieces of warm clothing, horse hobbles, and lengths of rope that began to get tangled around Beyaz' hind hooves. I was expecting him to lash out violently, then suddenly remembered the Turkish horse command for 'calm down' (which I'd heard in the market).

'*Sss-sssss-sss*,' I crooned at him. The effect was immediate and he came to a standstill. Now came the dodgy bit, I had to get under his belly to unfasten the saddlebag cinch, an area which needs caution with any strange horse.

Watching his hooves for the slightest twitch, and ss-ss-ing continually, I crouched by his legs and pulled the cinch undone. Luckily I've long learned that horse-tack fastenings must be instantly openable. The tack dropped free, and Beyaz stood quietly while I collected up my strewn possessions, and re-saddled him.

On the way back to Ürgüp the sky went dark and rain began lashing down. Darker still, the rain turned to hail, which stung my skin and made Beyaz try to put his back to its force. There was nowhere to shelter and since we were already soaked, I urged the pony to hurry home.

I felt frozen to the bone, and back in Ürgüp I put on all my warmest clothes, realising that what I'd intended to wear on the icy heights of Eastern Anatolia was only just enough at this level. That night I filled my drinking-water flask with boiling water to keep my feet warm.

The next day I rode north from Ürgüp. To the east I could see the summit of the snowclad volcano Erciyes, floating on top of some clouds. I followed the road until clear of town then took the earliest opportunity of branching away across country. Not that there had been much traffic, just an occasional *dolmuş* or pick-up truck, but their drivers blared their horns as they passed and none bothered to slacken speed or to give us space. When a tourist bus roared past, Beyaz sidled nervously, but even so, he was remarkably docile. The main reason I left the road was because I loathe riding along roads, they're constructed for vehicles, whereas a horse has four-hoof drive.

We passed a shepherd with his flock and Anatolian shepherd dog – not a sheepdog, this breed is large and powerful with a broad head and dense coat. His job was to protect the sheep not herd them, and I noticed he was wearing a fearsome spiked metal collar to stop wolves getting him by the throat. The dog didn't look too friendly either and I was glad to be on horseback.

Beyaz scurried along at a comfortable flat trot. The commands for 'go faster' are *ht* and *vt* or any sharp guttural sounds. From the rim of a low escarpment we went down among stubby pinnacles and across a plain towards the abandoned village of Zelve.

Old Zelve village was hewn from the rocky sides of three narrow valleys; it was abandoned after the rock began to collapse, killing some occupants. The Turkish government provided funds to build a new modern village and the people moved into it. Only the pigeons stayed on. Each family had owned five or six pigeon lofts, carved into the cliffs usually as the top room of each family house, and now more than ever the pigeons were flourishing.

I met an old man who had come back to feed his flock. He said all villagers do this in winter, and in return the birds provide eggs (most are left to hatch but some are eaten), droppings for fertiliser, and meat in the autumn. Pigeon kebab, he smacked his lips in appreciation and threw another handful of corn to the birds.

They fluttered down around him and one alighted on his shoulder, the man's weatherbeaten face creased into a smile and he pulled more corn from a leather pouch which hung on the string belt of his baggy trousers. On his head was a cloth cap; most Turkish men wear them. I'd also taken to wearing a cloth cap, as a convenient sunhat. I hadn't thought about it as a male disguise, but it was odd how villagers assumed I must be a man. With my blonde hair hidden from sight, my figure slim not shapely, it seldom occurred to men that a solo horse rider could be female. Even this old man called me *bey* (mister), though it was pretty obvious I was female when I spoke.

He showed me his old family house, empty but for the millwheel where a donkey had circled to grind corn, and the fireplace where the women had baked bread inside a sunken pottery jar. There were two upper storeys for the family and a lower cave that had been the stable for their donkeys and sheep. The raised entrance was a protection against raiders, and they had a round stone door to seal the opening in case of attack.

My companion led me through a tunnel into an adjoining valley, coming out down the back stairs of a church. Half the church has caved in but its ceiling still bears a painting of a deer. Other churches have fish and grape frescoes, and a four-storey monastery has collapsed leaving the rooms and chapels exposed in cross-section.

The old man grumbled when it was time for him to go back to the new village. The old houses, he said, were so much better, keeping cool in summer and warm in winter; their new concrete houses aren't half as good.

I continued riding north; hot sun, cold wind, it was exhilarating. An hour later we reached Sarihan, a Seljuk caravanserai dating from 1250, and one of the finest still surviving, though probably not the largest. There used to be caravanserais at fifty-kilometre intervals all along the ancient trade routes; any place whose name ends -han contained one. This was a route to Iran, Afghanistan and China.

Sari means orange, the colour of the stone used to build this caravanserai, although much of the outer stonework has been taken for local buildings. Classically square-walled, it encloses a large courtyard partly covered with arched stalls for animals; the superb craftsmanship of Seljuk stonemasonry incorporated three colours of stone into the arches. The vault of the entrance arch was straddled by a small mosque, and the arch itself was beautifully decorated with entwined geometric patterns in relief.

A large sleeping room for people and an even larger room for animals in winter meant there was space for about two caravans, the average caravan being twenty camels, eight men, three horses and a donkey or two. Water was provided through pottery pipes from a spring one kilometre distant.

Beyond Sarihan the land became flat and rather dull so I looped south back into wonderland. Storm clouds were circling the mountains again and it seemed prudent to be within reach of shelter; the foothills were ideal with their plentiful pinnacle rock houses and churches, unnamed and seldom visited except by shepherds. It is a shame that smoke from their fires has blackened the frescoes, but one can still recognise some of the pictures from glimpses of figures and their haloes.

While I stopped to eat on the bank of a stream a man came along. I saw him notice me and duck down to crouch watching me. Several minutes passed, and without appearing hasty I readied my gear for a quick getaway, should it be necessary, then I relaxed with my picnic of fresh bread, cheese and tomatoes. The man came closer and sat in full view near me, an unkempt youth; I don't know why he made me feel wary, perhaps it was the way he eyed my luggage. Nevertheless, I told myself sternly that it is normal behaviour for a man to be curious about finding a traveller. He refused to share my picnic, being Ramazan, but he answered my enquiry about his name and that of his village; such information is an insurance against trouble.

Meanwhile, Beyaz had espied my picnic and he sauntered over. No shifty glances, he had his beady eyes fixed on the bread. As he tried to snatch it I tapped him on the nose, he stepped back guiltily and to my amusement he nonchalantly pretended to eat some withered bits of grass-root just beside the bread. His eyes rolled with the effort of not losing sight of it, and even my surly acquaintance began to grin. I tucked the bread away but Beyaz was obsessed, even though the grazing was lush with young clover, so I saddled him and gave him the remains of the bread before moving off.

Later we reached a road and joined its traffic of horse and donkey-carts. The carts were wooden with the back wood-spoked wheels much larger than the front ones. Prestige carts had rubber tyres. The peasant women driving the carts were returning from their day's work in the fields, and as the storm clouds loomed overhead they began to increase their pace.

Beyaz was cantering on the verge, determined not to be overtaken by a mule. A two-horse team swung past at a gallop, their driver standing up to manage her team better and to avoid being jolted to pieces by the unsprung chassis.

Within minutes the cloud was dropping hailstones and the line of carts turned into something resembling a chariot race. I crouched over Beyaz's neck as he thundered along, the hail stung badly and the storm was growing worse.

In the gloom ahead I could see a village, and with a final sprint the racing carts hurtled into the village street. No celebration at the finishing post, everyone simply disappeared to shelter. I found a *çayevi* (teahouse) where Beyaz could fit under the roof, and revived myself with glasses of apple-flavoured tea.

Beyaz stumbled frequently on the way back to Ürgüp and, realising he had probably not had such an active two days for months, I gave him the next day off while I went alone to the underground city at Kaymakli.

Kaymakli lies on flat dull plateauland. It is an ordinary-seeming village, yet in a group of rocks there is a hole which is the entrance to a large subterranean city hollowed out in the sixth century by Christians who wanted a hiding place for their families.

A sign at the entrance said the place would close for an hour at midday, but I had my flashlight and thought it wouldn't matter if the electric lighting was turned off. Down and down narrow tunnels, stooping bent double, I found rooms had been hollowed at different levels with many passages and holes interlinking them. It was like being in a human ant colony. Some rooms had pits in the floor for jars of water, oil and wine. One room had pits for burying the dead. This city could house 15,000 people; it goes about twenty storeys down, though only the upper forty metres, or eight storeys, are open to the public. Some tunnels are not yet explored and there's reputed to be one leading to a second underground city nine kilometres away at Derinküyü.

Another underground city has recently been discovered in this area and probably others yet remain unknown. Their main purpose was to hide terrified Christians from hordes of militant Arab invaders. The area was hard to defend, no rocks for walls, the best defence lay in disappearance. The Christians had stored enough grain underground to last for years, although usually they only needed to hide for a week or two. Invaders finding a deserted village generally didn't stay around. A tunnel to the summit of a nearby hill provided the refugees with a lookout point to see when it was safe to re-emerge.

For ventilation and smoke from cooking fires there were other separate shafts. As I understood it, the city was built to a conical plan, a few rooms up top expanding to multitudes below; each storey had a kitchen attached to the same smoke shaft, and a toilet attached to a common waste shaft, while a third shaft was a well for the city's water supply.

Sliding along a tunnel between storeys I dropped my torch, it went out and wouldn't revive. The blackness was intense and I felt my way along for a while groping with feet and hands. The tunnel eventually linked with a well-lit trodden path and I wasn't afraid of getting lost. Echoes came from other parties in the city, growing fewer, then I heard the departing shouts of the last group and suddenly the city fell silent.

It occurred to me that the lights would probably now go out, in which case I would be stuck for a while and unable to find my way out. But doubtless more people would arrive in the afternoon, no need to panic. The emptiness was wonderful. I tried to imagine how the inhabitants had found their way around with oil lamps. Small sleeping cubicles were hollowed beside family caverns, and the stables for livestock were complete with stone mangers. Finally I emerged back at ground level, into blinding sunlight.

From Kaymakli I hitch-hiked to the even larger buried city at Derinküyü, and thence east, chancing to get a lift with a Turkish acquaintance from Ürgüp called Aydin. He suggested a visit to Soganli village thirty-five kilometres away, to which I agreed since Soganli is off the main tourist route and it has a concentration of fine frescoes.

Near Soganli we looked at the paintings in the Church of Serpents. Despite its smoke-blackening I could make out St George fighting the dragon; the Last Judgement; and Abraham, Isaac and Jacob holding the children of Israel's twelve tribes. Another church we saw had scenes of the Nativity and the first bath of the infant Jesus. At the head of the valley Aydin pointed out a footpath on the opposite side of the valley and said he would meet me in Soganli, so I continued on foot.

The path led to a domed church with many tiny chambers and then to a lower hidden church, hidden because your eyes are distracted by the chambers above with their alcoves and paintings in grey and orange. But if you go around the back and push open a wood door, you enter a lovely arched church with pillars and side aisles.

The walk was a pleasure; abundant daisies, grape-hyacinths, and church ruins. It felt good to stretch my muscles, stiff from two days on horseback. The air carried the sounds of donkeys braying and pigeons cooing. In Soganli I found Aydin drinking tea with a man who had just finished hewing two new rooms out of rock. Their walls were still soft and crumbly, and the man told me it would take a year for the rock to become dry and hard. For the work of excavation he had been helped by the village expert. Every village has some professional excavators whose knowledge is hereditary. The work is highly skilled, a sculpture from the inside; if the walls have thin patches they will be eroded by rain and snow. It had taken the two men six months to hollow out the two rooms with a floor area of seventy square metres.

The drive back to Ürgüp took us past vineyards and orchards, and up on to a treeless, windswept rocky plateau at 2,700 metres, before descending into a landscape of rugged cliffs and conical chimneys. We passed a ruined caravanserai, and villages with mosques eye-catching by their needle-like minarets. Between villages were fields of onion and garlic, tomatoes, aubergines, paprika, and orchards of apricots, peaches and cherries, still very unripe.

At Mustafapaşa, Aydin stopped to show me around, explaining that this was once a Greek town, before Atatürk expelled the Greeks and implanted Selonic people. The tall square houses with wooden shutters and wrought ironwork balconies looked wealthier than Turkish houses, which had probably been true, since part of the antagonism between Turks and Greeks was because the Greeks worked hard and grew rich.

Back in Ürgüp, Aydin and I had supper together, although it wasn't yet sunset and he was nervous in case any acquaintance saw him eating. He hadn't been keeping Ramazan, I had already seen him drinking tea and smoking, but he was pretending to his family and friends. Some men came into the café to stare at the food; Aydin said they would break Ramazan within a week. Here in Ürgüp it was less strict, being a tourist place, but most towns were rigid and there were cases of offenders being whipped for eating or even smoking in public.

The following day I collected Beyaz for a ride; a late start, townspeople were up and about, and they greeted me, 'What again!' 'Where are you going today?' My simple reply was '*Gesiorum*' which means to wander randomly. No two valleys were the same, and somehow I never tired of that region; in a rocky outcrop near Çemil I found a hideout and monastery built by the Greeks. Its entrance was obscured by a rocky overhang, and on further inspection I realised that the whole outcrop had been honeycombed: one room had a bread oven, another a rack for spit-roasting a sheep, nooks for soup jars and cooking pots, and the back room had ceiling hooks made of rock, which people had used for butchering the sheep. There was a church with superb frescoes, and a tunnel to Çemil, two kilometres away.

Discoveries like these made each day an adventure. But I

decided not to buy Beyaz, my heart was craving something wilder. And in the way that journeys create themselves, this one needed to broaden its perspective, and build up some mileage, before it could go deep.

Gesiorum – an excellent Turkish word for my next instalment of travels. Pressing further north-east towards what I felt would be the most exciting part of Turkey, I caught a bus to Erzurum where the Anatolian Plateau crumples into a volcanic upheaval of peaks and valleys. The mountains were snowy, the sleet lashed down and we drove towards an ever-retreating rainbow. When I asked a fellow passenger what the bus's speed limit was he replied, 'Speed limit? I suppose it is death.'

Erzurum was full of promise, but as I sat in the *otogar*, or bus station, sipping hot sweet tea at 6 a.m., I realised I had arrived too soon. There was heavy snow still on the mountains through which I hoped to ride on horseback and, of course, it was still Ramazan. In short, I would be cold and hungry. At this point of realisation the thing is not to curse one's lack of forward planning, but to do something about it.

What I did was get back on a bus and take a week-long sickle sweep south to the heat of the Syrian border and west to the coastal cities of former Greek colonies. It wasn't where I had planned to be, but I wouldn't have missed the sacred fish pond of Abraham at Urfa in the upper Tigris basin, or hunting for the lost ruins of the port of Kyme along the Aegean coast, or the dervish called Ismail who practised his English on me in Istanbul.

When I got back to Erzurum summer was still a month away from eastern Anatolia, but this gave me a good opportunity to fit in a journey across the border into Iran. I had already obtained a visa. By the time I came back both winter and Ramazan would be over.

Before leaving Erzurum I made a new friend, a young woman called Sema. I was looking for the Tourist Office and with my still imperfect Turkish found myself laying siege to the Agricultural Office by mistake. It was Sema who fielded me in good working English and immediately I knew I had met a kindred spirit in that most unlikely of eastern towns. Sema was holding down a responsible job in the Department of Agriculture and did not veil her face or even wear a headscarf. When I explained my plans to go into Iran she warned me that it had a bad name, but offered to mind my excess luggage for me and I looked forward to seeing her again on my return to Turkey in a month's time.

Two

FROM CASPIAN COAST TO DESERT OF SALT

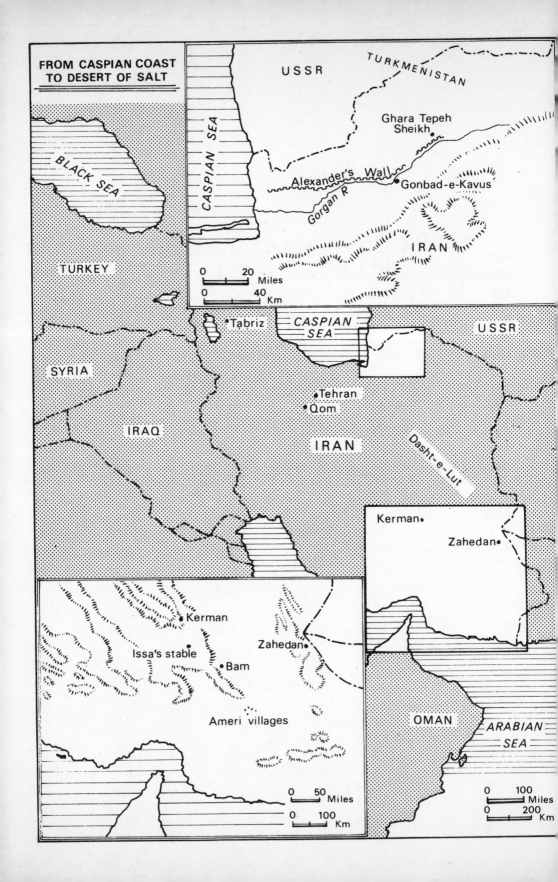

FROM CASPIAN COAST
TO DESERT OF SALT

USSR

TURKMENISTAN

Ghara Tepeh
Sheikh

Alexander's   Wall

Gorgan R

Gonbad-e-Kavus

IRAN

BLACK
SEA

TURKEY

0   20
|‾‾|‾‾|‾‾|‾‾| Miles
0   40
|‾‾|‾‾|‾‾|‾‾| Km

Tabriz

CASPIAN
SEA

USSR

SYRIA

Tehran
Qom

IRAN

IRAQ

Dasht-e-Lut

Kerman

Zahedan

Kerman

Issa's stable

Bam

Zahedan

Ameri villages

OMAN

ARABIAN
SEA

0   50
|‾‾|‾‾|‾‾| Miles
0   100
|‾‾|‾‾|‾‾| Km

0   100
|‾‾|‾‾|‾‾| Miles
0   200
|‾‾|‾‾|‾‾| Km

2   A guarded welcome to Iran

How would Iran be different from Turkey, I wondered? People had warned me that Ramazan is stricter, and I had been given conflicting advice about whether or not as a foreigner to wear a *chadoor*, the black tent-like garment that Iranian women put on over their normal clothes when they go out in public. Some people said it would be necessary for me to wear one, others said it would look suspiciously as though I were trying to disguise myself. So I put on a long-sleeved shirt, trousers, socks, and took a large drab brown headscarf in case of need.

My visa for Iran was a transit one which meant that I had to leave by a different border from where I entered, and since the only two open road frontiers seemed to be at Maku from Turkey and at Zahedan into Pakistan, this simplified matters. I could go to Pakistan and renew my transit visa for coming back across Iran.

This would give me an extendable month in Iran, two sets of two weeks, and I decided that rather than wasting my time drifting along main roads, I would choose four or five areas and spend up to a week in each. The places I chose were the Turkoman tribal region east of Gonbad-e-Kavus and the Caspian Sea, which was where my only contact in Iran was living; the valleys of the Assassins to the south of the Caspian Sea; Kurdistan; the environs of Shiraz, Persepolis, and the Qashgai tribal centre of Firuzabad; and the southern deserts around Kerman and Bam. These places should show me a good cross-section of life in Iran, and keep me out of the war zones. I don't believe in deliberately looking for trouble, one finds enough of that in the normal course of a journey; and from people's reactions when I told them I was going to Iran, it seemed that this was enough of a risk for a solo Western woman.

When I reached the border post the atmosphere was rather surly so I put on my headscarf. All the other women were swathed in *chadoors*, leaving only their eyes and nose showing.

To reach the Iranian side of the border I had to walk for a couple of kilometres. The mud on the road was deeper than my shoes, which gave me oozing socks, but before long I was sitting in a road-works caravan drinking illicit tea, while trying to find out about onward buses.

From the nearby town of Maku, buses run to Tabriz and Tehran. Tabriz didn't interest me at this stage, because I could stop there on the way back, so I bought a ticket on the next bus to Tehran which gave me five hours to spare in Maku and I passed the time looking for the cave that is reputed to be large enough to hold three thousand men.

Maku is set in a cliff-sided gorge and caves are plentiful. I rambled around up the back of the town and at lunchtime I found a secluded spot for my picnic. But people kept coming up to stare at me and ask what I was doing. I felt as though I was turning into a secret eater.

Some nomadic women strolled over in gaudy full-skirted dresses, headbands and glittery gold scarves, making a contrast to all the other black hooded crows. Maybe it's the way the women pull the black cloth over their forehead in a beak-shape that makes me think of birds, wings folded or flapping as they walk around. Usually they carry their shopping bags inside the *chadoor*, and if they have no spare hand, they hold the front of the *chadoor* closed with their teeth.

The bus left punctually and the road followed Maku's gorge as it gradually widened to a broad valley between superb escarpments. Stark outcrops of red rock jutted out of a desert carpeted with springtime flowers. We drove through a snow-storm, big wet flakes, and moments later watched dustdevils spinning. There were a few hamlets of flat-roofed mud houses inhabited by semi-nomadic people whose herds of sheep, goats and horses grazed nearby.

This is geographically a corridor between the Zagros Mountains, running in numerous parallel folds that fill western Iran, and the Elburz range which arches around the south Caspian coastline. Iran's interior is a triangular dish of upland plateau whose form reflects its origin as a sea bed. From the mountains, rivers drain into the desert bringing fertile alluvial silt. But beyond the fertile arc there are vast arid deserts of sand and salt. Three thousand years ago, warring hordes swept into the arable parts from the Central Asian steppes in search of new pastures for their flocks. Powers waxed and waned, though generally Iran has absorbed her conquerors, like a great cultural sponge, which re-shapes those who go there.

The area I was heading for is not typical of Iran scenically, being at the Caspian Sea's south-east shore, a hinterland where Iran borders Russia. It is a Turkoman enclave of steppeland with scattered groups of mountains. No great trade routes took people there, no great explorers passed through, it sounded lost and forgotten. Just my sort of place.

Meanwhile, military road blocks were frequent and the bus had to wait while soldiers came aboard to check passengers and baggage. They didn't seem concerned with me, and I wasn't worried because I'd been told that soldiers and police are generally sensible and helpful, it's only the Revolutionary Guards who make trouble. They can be recognised because most of them have beards. Soldiers also flagged the bus down in isolated points in the desert to commandeer seats for wounded men with blood-stained bandages, a sobering reminder that the Iran – Iraq war was in its seventh year.

At the truckers' inn where we stopped for supper I had problems because I couldn't read the Farsi script of the meal-tickets, so I went into the kitchen and indicated some rice and kebab but couldn't read the money to pay for it. Back outside I couldn't even identify my bus, all destinations were written in Farsi. But some of the road signs had translations in our alphabet, and one large billboard read 'Down with America', illustrated by gory pictures of what the Iranian militants would like to do to America with bayonets. My fellow-passengers asked me what country I came from. I felt uncomfortable saying Britain, it's not popular either, so I added that I'd spent ten years in Africa.

And I began discovering some of the multiple uses of a headscarf or *chadoor*; to shield my face from the dust, to avoid people's stares, and to cover my face when I wanted to go to sleep.

At 6 a.m. we arrived in Tehran, in time for me to catch the early bus to Gonbad-e-Kavus, nine hours away. The road goes past Mount Damavand, and there is a legend of a giant who sits trapped inside the mountain, looking with one eye at the past and the other gazing at the future. Snowdrifts lay near the road as we rose high into the Elburz Mountains bordering the Caspian Sea. Rock strata have been twisted and thrust up in perpendicular cliffs. But the crash bars along the road had been torn from their sockets and lay strewn in the valleys below alongside wrecked vehicles.

This is an historic traffic route. I spotted a castle of the Assassins who used to take a toll from trade caravans using the route, if they didn't rob them bare. The castle's walls looked intact, situated on a cliff-sided outcrop halfway up the valley. Descending from the heights towards the inland sea, which is about twenty metres below sea level, there was a sudden dramatic change from barren arid mountains to jungly trees and rice paddies, water buffalo, lush greenness and yellow irises. The air became hot and clammy. But I didn't dare roll up my shirtsleeves, for my neighbour had already told me off for not wearing a *chadoor*.

We drove along the Caspian shore. The water has receded and is hardly visible from the road, the shore line now being oozy mud. Fishermen were selling sturgeon by the road and I noted a caviar processing factory nearby. Tribeswomen had set up roadside stalls for passing trade to buy their baskets, wooden spoons, jugs and ornaments. But there was no forgetting the war. A town we passed through was decorated with photographs of their war-dead, volunteer victims, all along the main street, many looked not much older than children. One café was open in that street, despite Ramazan, though newspaper had been plastered over the windows to prevent anyone seeing who was inside.

Way before we reached Gonbad-e-Kavus I could see the tower-tomb which gives the town its name – Tomb of Kavus. Robert Byron, that suave and scholarly traveller of the thirties, described the tomb-tower as one of the four most beautiful structures in Iran. The body of King Kavus had once been suspended in a glass coffin within this tall pencil of brick. He was revered for his kindness and wisdom, but was killed by his son. Since Robert Byron's visit, the tomb's brickwork has been pockmarked by the bullets of a battle six years ago during the revolution, when counter-revolutionaries seized the town.

I had come to Gonbad partly to see the famous tomb, but also because it was the nearest town to the ranch of Narcy and Louise Firouz to whom I had been given an introduction by an Iranian-born friend in London. Now I found the road leading out toward their village of Ghara Tepeh Sheikh and a car stopped to offer me a lift. But as I climbed in, a van with siren wailing tore up and screeched to a halt across the road. Bearded men grabbed hold of my arms and pushed me into their van. They threw my backpack in after me and with sirens still wailing drove to the headquarters of the Revolutionary Guards.

We parked in a prisoners' exercise yard and I was hauled over towards the cells. My protests and resistance met with rough treatment; the guards shoved me over to a cell door and unlocked it.

Inside was dimly lit through a barred window; it was a tiny cell with four dirty bunk beds, already occupied by three women who cowered back in fear. Every fibre in my body screamed NO, but things were happening so fast I hardly knew how to react. Whatever the penalty, I wasn't going into that cell, suspecting that once you're locked inside it's easy for people to forget you're there.

'Take off your shoes,' the guard indicated I must leave my sandals outside the door.

'First tell me what I've done wrong,' I requested.

'No, take off your shoes,' he snapped back. So I bent down and unbuckled one sandal, then stood up and asked to speak to the boss. 'No,' he yelled, 'take off your shoes.' After slipping one sandal off I tried a fresh protest, which met with some expletives in Farsi. So I put one sandal back on and took the other one off, trying a new argument between each move. I was playing for time, hoping that someone might see us from an office window and intervene.

Eight times I managed to take off one shoe and put on the other! Then just as the guard lost his temper an officer appeared, and he beckoned us back into the exercise yard. There he searched my handbag and confiscated my passport and the dictionary of Farsi words that I had been trying to build up. (It had been impossible to buy a Farsi dictionary written in western alphabet, so I had begun making one in a notebook.) 'That's not incriminating,' I said. 'Look, these words are mother, father, house, village.' But the officer couldn't read my alphabet and he seemed to think I was lying. He couldn't speak English, none of them knew more than 'No' and 'Take off your shoes', and without my dictionary I couldn't speak any Farsi. They locked me in a solitary cubicle which adjoined a row of cells, and left me to stew for four hours.

My mind was in turmoil, going from bewilderment to anger and down to despair. There was one brief interruption when a guard came in but he wouldn't tell me why I was being held, and he refused my request to telephone my ambassador. Although the British no longer have an embassy in Iran I knew that British problems are handled by the Swedish Embassy. It seemed I had no rights at all.

Later another guard came in carrying a prison dress, which he told me to put on, but I refused politely saying that I'd not come to stay. He left me to stew again, clanging the door and locking it behind him.

This time I was more active, and by talking through the grille of one of the adjoining cells I located a male prisoner who could speak some English. I explained that when an opportunity arose he must ask on my behalf why I was under arrest. Outside the daylight faded into night.

Mosquitoes arose in clouds. Supper time came: bread and soup. I refused to eat but the men in the next cell asked if I would mind giving them my share, so I slid the bowl in under their grille.

And such was my welcome to Iran.

At exercise time all the male prisoners were released into the yard. Some uniformed men were standing to one side, and I called to my English-speaking ally, 'Please ask now.'

This led to me being taken out for interrogation, with my ally as translator, and finally the problem became clear. When I had entered Iran the frontier police had stamped an extra piece of paper with my entry details, and these Revolutionary Guards had noticed the police stamp and assumed that I'd been in trouble with the police.

The officer waved the paper at me, I explained it was a frontier formality, and suddenly they all began to laugh. My arrest had been a mistake. They apologised and asked me not to think badly of Iran. Would I like some tea and sweet pastries?

Before releasing me they said I would be wise to wear a *chadoor* or its alternative, the *mantau*, a cloth coat that buttons at wrists, neck and reaches below the knees. Other bearded guards took me to a hotel and, still treating me like a convict, told the manager to call them if I tried to leave. That's not what I term 'released'. My room looked much like a cell, and mosquitoes plagued me all night.

Early the next morning I argued my way out the door to buy bread, leaving my backpack as hostage at the hotel; but no bread was available, being Ramazan. There was a final argument when I checked out of the hotel, but I stormed away in a temper and no one gave chase, then I hitched a lift into the countryside towards my friends' village. After about thirty kilometres I left that ride and found another but was stopped by a fortified outpost of Revolutionary Guards.

'Gonbad. Telephone Gonbad,' I said insistently and made a show of indignation. They searched my luggage item by item, and let me go. The land was level grassy steppe, now growing wheat, and I could see isolated flat-topped mounds that looked like unexcavated fortresses and settlements. Locally the mounds are called *tepeh*. This whole area is little excavated. The last ten kilometres to the village were along rutted dirt roads, it seemed a remote place for a family to live.

3 Caspian miniatures and Alexander's Wall

In London, my Iranian friend Roshan Reddaway had said I would love her mother. Louise is an American woman who went to Iran as a bride in 1957 and has lived there ever since. She and her husband, Narcy Firouz, are ranchers. Just outside their village, Ghara Tepeh Sheikh, I came to their barn.

Roshan was there on holiday with her young son Alex and she introduced me to Louise and Narcy. They gave me a lovely welcome and tea on the *talar*, a raised platform of bamboo covered in Turkoman felt rugs, open to the breeze and shaded by a thatched roof on poles. There was a bowl of roses on the rugs and we relaxed there drinking tea and munching bread and honey.

With this open-air living room they have no house, though in rainy weather they inhabit a room at the end of the horses' barn. But there is no electricity, no fridge, nor running water. Water from the nearby river is poured into their small round reservoir, which is also the horses' drinking trough, and Alex's paddling pool. He said he had a pet whale in it. Drinking water is stored separately to let the mud settle. Louise and Narcy have lived here for fourteen years and have no great quarrel with this self-sufficient life, farming an acre of land, and breeding a few horses.

Revived by the tea, Roshan and I went out horse-riding across a plain of wheat which was ripening from green to gold. The plain is bisected by narrow mud canyons that you can't see until you are on top of their edge. We rode along a tributary arm and down into another watershed.

My mount was a half-bred Turkoman mare that Louise had found pulling a sesame seed oil press round and round. The mare was a little highly strung but easily controllable. We waded through a shallow stream where brown frogs with vivid green-striped backs leaped aside. Young cotton was growing on the stream banks, and among the herds of fat-tailed sheep in a Turkoman village, turkeys were being used to hatch broods of ducklings. Ducks are often bad egg-sitters.

Turkomans are a semi-nomadic tribe who originated in the Central Asian steppes, archetypal nomad warriors and horse-breeders. Their land, Turkmenistan, was annexed by Russia in 1881 and even now the majority of Turkomans live in Russia. Some of the men we met wore fur hats with sheep's wool ringlets hanging in curls to frame their flat slant-eyed faces. Turkoman women don't wear the *chadoor*, just headscarves, and in another village I saw them dressed in raw-silk knee length kaftans with embroidered necks and different coloured linings. Beneath their kaftans they wore floral cotton trousers, very gathered at the waist and joined on to pieces of richly embroidered cloth, decorating the lower legs below the kaftan. The smartest lady's kaftan had side panels ornamented with silver medallions, brooches, chains and buttons.

The goal of our ride was a Turkoman village famed for its racehorses. A typical Turkoman racehorse is long-backed, 15-15.2 hands high, and the Byerley-Turkoman is one of the three ancestors of the thoroughbred. The stamina of Turkoman racehorses is legendary, for until recently they were ridden on long plundering raids of up to 200 kilometres into foreign territory. Stamina was necessary for making a quick getaway. The horses were sometimes fed meat. Their training was said to involve gallops of a hundred kilometres, and if the horse needed to drink water afterwards, it was not good enough. These horses have adapted to dryness. Now they need very little water, and, being springtime when I was there, the grass was succulent.

Felts are another speciality of Turkoman horse-breeders. Most of the horses we saw were wrapped in them. It seemed a curious idea to blanket horses in summer but people assured me that this is a Turkoman tradition and many thick layers of felt can keep a horse cool in the summer heat. When horses are ridden in felts they sweat easily, the moisture is soaked up by the first layer of felt which then acts in any slight breeze as a cooling agent. Sweating off the fat also keeps the horses' shape narrow and comfortable to ride. Other felts would be tied under the horse's belly to prevent it being pestered by flies.

We watched felts being prepared. Two girls were beating piles of sheep's wool with pairs of long sticks, to break it up. Later it would be pressed into flat pieces and laid out as a

blanket in layers of flat wodges, mingling white and black wool
to make a pattern. Boiling water is next poured on to the wool
and the girls press it with their forearms to compact it into felt.

Back at Ghara Tepeh Sheikh we went to tea in the village, a
special invitation since the villagers loved blond little Alex, and
he and Roshan were only visiting for ten days. Tea was in the
cottage of a woman who has three daughters and was given a
son by related villagers. The eldest daughter was beautiful with
an oval face and slanting almond eyes; she was sitting at a
horizontal loom making a carpet, threading its knots in the
customary Persian way between three rows; ends coming up
in two rows with a loop around the third. One girl was making
a prayer carpet, another was knotting covers for floor cushions,
following traditional red and black patterns. The design on one
of the finished rugs incorporated the motif of the Gonbad-e-
Kavus.

The girls knew the patterns by heart, so identified with their
craft that it seemed they wove their mood and thoughts into
each carpet. The speed of their fingers was astonishing; I'd
heard that an average weaver can do 8,000 knots a day, though
a record of 19,000 was claimed by an Armenian woman. Inter-
mittently the girls would thud the knots solid with a wooden
comb, and they sheared the carpet top after every few lines. I
have never understood the tourist passion for acquiring carpets
and rugs on one's travels. But here, I realised, carpets are
special. They are a status symbol, measuring wealth and prestige by their number and quality, and in a nomadic world, as
the proverb says, 'Where lies thy carpet, is thine home.'

Roshan said that the villagers speak Farsi with an American
accent – using Turkoman at home and Farsi with Louise! We
had refills of tea, no spoons, you put the sugar lump in your
mouth and drink the tea through it.

The villagers believe in *djinn*, spirits of good and evil. Every
home is full of *djinn*, who can look after themselves, but their
babies are vulnerable. When villagers accidentally kill *djinn*
babies, there is trouble. I noticed that when some boiling tea
was thrown out of the door, the woman muttered 'Bis-mi-lah'
(in the name of God) to protect the *djinn* babies. And most
Iranians use the expression 'Masallah' to avert the evil eye,
rather like we say 'touch wood'. I had to adapt to local customs,
the women would teach me; they did it to help me behave
correctly and not cause offence or be blamed for an accident.

As we were leaving, we stopped to greet a man who had recently arrived herding his sheep from the mountains. He was setting up his *alachekh* beside the village. An *alachekh* is a tent. When travellers in Central Asia brought back the word *yurt* they mistook its meaning. *Yurt* means the ground on which the *alachekh* is pitched.

The womenfolk were tying the framework of poles, using the same design as I'd previously seen among the Kazakhs of north-west China. They bound the joins with string and began covering the whole structure, except for the smoke-hole at the top, with several layers of felt which is naturally waterproof. The poles are protected from rot by a layer of soot, which also seems to keep them strong. Against the sooted and dusty felts the women stood out in long brightly coloured dresses and several layers of loosely hanging headscarves. The scarves are draped over a cardboard ring on top of each woman's head. Perhaps the custom comes from the advantages of letting one's hair breathe.

The horses were still out grazing when we arrived back at the barn. Tethered by the *talar* was a miniature horse, only eleven h.h. but perfectly proportioned. Louise told me that it was a Caspian, an ancient breed of miniature horse which had been extinct for 1,500 years, and is considered by many to be the missing link in the evolution of the horse, far pre-dating the ancient Arab.

Although Louise didn't tell me the whole story at once, I pieced it together as our friendship developed. A remarkable woman, she had been responsible for reviving the breed which had died out in Sassanian times. Occasionally, even today, an ordinary mare in foal will produce a genetic throwback to ancient stock, whose proportions and characteristics are identical to the miniature Caspian horse of the Achaemenians, as depicted on the walls of Darius the Great's palace at Persepolis, and on a trilingual seal a pair of them are shown pulling his hunting chariot. From the bones Louise has seen, she estimates that the typical Caspian was eleven hands high, with some as small as nine hands, less than a metre to the shoulder.

Next morning Louise and I went riding north-west towards the Russian border and as we rode she explained how she had first discovered the Caspians. Back in 1965 when she was looking for ponies for her children, Iran's normal choice being only between obstinate donkeys and spirited plateau stallions, she ventured over the Elburz Mountains towards the Caspian Sea where she had once noticed a pony-sized horse. In the fertile lowland crescent by the sea she had found a small bay stallion, but the more she looked at him the more she was puzzled, he did not look like a pony, his proportions were perfect for a horse. A pony's proportions are different, sturdier with a thicker body and shorter legs. From a photograph with no point of scale, it could be difficult to tell the Caspian isn't a full-sized horse. By a village in reed swamps Louise found an even smaller chestnut stallion and she realised that the first bay was not a unique phenomenon.

'Caspian horses are easy to identify in the wild, even at a distance,' Louise said, 'because of the way they trot, moving more like a deer than a horse. This accounts for their fabulous jumping ability. But in the wild state they're vicious and will strike with forelegs, kick and bite. Though they aren't difficult to tame and since they're so bright they learn quickly.' Louise had begun to establish her foundation herd twenty years ago. It sometimes seemed a losing task as every year the already small numbers were reduced by famine and sickness. But what had started as an idle search for children's ponies had become a long fascination.

Louise found that the Caspian gene is strong and breeding has a good success rate. Her herd reached its peak at thirty horses and she worked to establish the breed internationally, presenting a mare and stallion to HRH Prince Philip on his visit to Iran for the 2,500-year celebrations. Breeding studs for Caspians now exist in England, Australia, New Zealand, Canada and the USA. But the typical Caspian changes when bred in a foreign stud, on different diet and minerals, and where the horse is used for skurry-racing, its breeding requirements are slightly different. So purity is not always maintained outside Iran.

This is not the world's only breed of miniature horse. My mother, who was raised in China, had owned a Szechwan miniature, and there are a few others. Now, although the Caspian breed has been re-established, it is threatened again. Seven years ago at the start of the Revolution, Louise lost much of her herd, while the Caspian breeding programme she had instigated through the Iranian Horse Society closed down. There was a ban on ownership of horses, nationalisation of all existing horses, and the Caspian mares were allowed to cross-breed back into the ordinary genetic melting-pot.

But Louise still seeks out the true Caspian genes, the tiny short hooves, fine bones, bold eyes, very small ears which curve inward at the tips, and high tail carriage like an Arab's. Herds of wild horses roam the mountains and steppes, spending summer in the high ground and coming down in winter to graze on the rice stubble, where they are rounded up annually, and identified by their owners. Louise found a golden filly this year, located her owner and bought her. The family called her Pari, which means Angel, in the hope that she would live up to her name.

Pari was tethered to the *talar* when we arrived back, learning to be calm around people. Louise and I turned our horses out into the paddock and finished preparing a lunch of *chakdameh*, a Turkoman dish whose main ingredients are lamb and rice cooked in the lamb juice, with bread and *mast* (yoghurt). Iranian food is far tastier than I had expected.

Taming and training the little mare progressed over the following days. She was saddled and given more affection, though we had to watch out for those front hooves. I went riding in the early mornings, heading south across the Gorgan River. I noted hoopoes, swallows, bee-eaters, kestrels, sparrows, crested meadow larks and finches overhead, and underfoot were turtles and slow-worms.

On one of my rides I found some pieces of pottery. The family had made a chart and collection of pottery fragments on the barn's end wall in order to learn which cultures had lived in their area. The shards were identified in groups that began with prehistoric painted pottery, reddish brown with black stripes; the second group, Iron Age, could be recognised by its black finish and grooves; while the Parthian (150 BC-AD 226) was dull brown clay. Louise had already taken me across the valley to look at the remains of some Parthian terracing and irrigation. The fourth group was Sassanid (AD 226-640), brown but decorated with lines; and this was followed by early Islamic pottery (AD 800-1000) in glazed blues, greens and brown.

An unexcavated *tepeh* that we often passed out riding was the mound of Ghara Tepeh; from the pottery Louise has found here she estimates it was inhabited between 8000 and 7000 BC. Standing on top of the mound makes your skin shiver into goosepimples. Somewhere around here is the undiscovered city of Sharakoumis, built by Alexander the Great as a garrison to establish control over a newly conquered area. He spent a winter in these parts, encouraged his soldiers to marry locally, and himself married Roxana, daughter of a defeated Bactrian chief. But the city he founded here has not yet been unearthed.

Riding back, Roshan pointed out Alexander's Wall, which I had seen marked in my world atlas, and while she and young Alex followed the track back to the village, I swung my white mare, Agh Baital, north-west to go and see it. Alexander's Wall is now only a long raised mound in a straight line with the shallow dip of a moat along one side. The bricks had been made of baked earth, but were long ago taken for house-building because they were good quality and much larger than our western bricks; the kilns for baking them had been set in arched fire holes all along the wall. Alexander, or Iskander, is not an uncommon name in Persia and Alexander the Great had nothing to do with building this wall, which was originally made circa 500 BC and rebuilt by the Sassanians to keep out invading hordes from the steppes and to enclose a sweet-water area. Beyond it the streams are brackish.

I went for a long gallop beside the wall's foundations. Agh Baital's huge strides thundered along, disturbing a wild pig which scuttled for cover in the wheat. I could see where boars had been rampaging and flattening the corn. This one was now racing through the tall wheat; but it wasn't fleeing, it was coming straight at us. Agh Baital reared up in a panic as the boar shot within a few metres of us, she hadn't seen it coming; we were all going so fast there was no time for me to do more than grab the horse's mane as she reared. The boar looked equally startled, it leapt over the wall-mound and vanished into long grass. People here don't hunt the wild pigs since pork is forbidden to Moslems, but some of them know that boar is delicious, and they can be prescribed it for treatment of certain stomach ailments.

We continued along the wall for a few kilometres then trotted back, because the mare wanted to gallop and by opting for a trot, she produced a superb extended pace. I loved the openness, the enormity of blue sky, combining with the vastness of time all around.

After lunch that day Louise brought out a bag of Bronze Age pot shards and we tried to stick them together again. Louise began working from the base of a little dish, while I took some more curved pieces. It was like doing a three-dimensional jigsaw, trying to match the curve and the incised design, and there was a real thrill in sticking six bits together. The fragments were an oxidised green copper colour, too thin and brittle to be pottery. Our Uhu glue, though comparatively antique, was still effective.

As we worked Louise talked about her life here as a rancher, when the ranch had been much bigger with a total herd of eighty horses. Winters were often hard. In one month they lost three donkeys, three Caspians and a bigger horse to a pack of wolves within three hundred metres of the stables. She and Narcy used to go on wolf-hunts, once in company with a revelling local wedding party. Another winter Louise took sixty horses and thirty sheep for refuge in a village in Kurdistan.

'What happened here during the Revolution?' My question got the flippant answer, 'Oh, Narcy and I were here, growing potatoes.' But slowly the real story came out: the barn had been attacked by Revolutionary Guards but they were beaten off by friendly Turkomans. Louise had broken an ankle as she and friends were running from bullets in the streets of Tehran and, returning to the village she had been arrested on suspicion of being a counter-revolutionary, for Gonbad was seized by counter-revolutionaries at this time and received the battle scars which I'd seen in town. When Louise was released back to the ranch she found her Caspian horses dying through neglect and malnutrition, and she herself was still under constant threat. It was the villagers who had protected her by saying, 'She's one of us.'

At the weekend Louise and I went off by jeep for an hour's drive towards the Russian border, to see an *alachekh* Louise had bought in order to expand their living quarters. Looking at the tent in situ would make it easier to reconstruct back near the barn.

After driving over Alexander's Wall Louise pointed out various mounds. 'That's where local people fought a pitched battle a few years ago. It was during the land wars, after the Revolution when people started trying to grab confiscated land. This flat bit is where my village fought using a tractor to charge at the enemy. The enemy also had a tractor, they charged full tilt at each other. Unfortunately at the vital moment, my village's tractor ran out of gas.'

One time when Louise drove up this way she had got lost and crossed into Russia. A soldier had finally stopped her and explained she was in Russia, but he admitted that the border sign had blown down and the frontier guards had not bothered to stand it up again because none of the local people could read anyway.

Reaching the *alachekh* we were invited in for tea and local bread with sheep's butter. Although the *alachekh* had been sold to Louise by an old lady and her sons, Louise would not remove it yet because it was the old lady's home. Frail and ill, the dying matriarch lay on a quilt, her skin so gaunt it shone like pale parchment. A daughter-in-law made the tea, her baby was asleep in a hammock slung from the tent's frame, and a larger grandchild was pulling a string to rock the hammock.

Sugar for our tea was cut from a solid cone of sugar, much denser than our sugar lumps. To cut it they use a strong metal pincer on a wooden stand; they prefer this type of compacted sugar because it doesn't dissolve too quickly in the mouth while one drinks the tea through it. Two men came in to consult their mother; I liked the way they honoured her, still asking her opinions and taking her orders for everyday activity.

I noticed some bamboo flutes, and the men offered to play them for me; the flutes were half a metre long with four holes on top and one at the bottom; the men said the flutes could be any length so long as they contained exactly seven segments of bamboo. The warbling tune revived their old mother who sat up and began spinning wool on a hand-spindle. Despite her frailty her eyes were bright and alert, and she listened with interest to our conversation. The story of my arrest in Gonbad gave great delight, and it increased my prestige enormously.

As we left, Louise checked how the tent was pitched, so that it would look the same when set up outside the barn. It would be more homely than the barn-end. Louise and Narcy seemed just as nomadic as the Turkoman who were only here to pasture their animals, and would migrate when the river dried up completely for the summer. In fact Louise and Narcy had another ranch near the valleys of the Assassins and I looked forward to visiting them there on my way back to Turkey.

Being me, I wanted to see where Alexander's Wall went inland. According to the atlas and the archaeologists it stopped after 150 kilometres. But the Turkomans said it ran all the way to Mashhad if you knew where to look for it, and some claimed their forebears had said it went right on to Afghanistan, plunging down steep mountains and up the other side, following a line that could be defended.

Louise was as enthusiastic as I to trace the wall further, and a Turkoman grandfather called Elias volunteered to be our guide, although nowadays, he warned, there is little to see but the line where the foundations had been.

So we three jumped in the jeep and drove along the line of the wall. Crested meadowlarks flew up from the track in front of our rattling approach, and the wheat was alive with turquoise bee-eaters and white butterflies. Nearing a village the line of the wall was barely visible since all the bricks had been long taken.

On the other side of the village we walked through the remains of a large fort, a garrison on a raised earth mound at the edge of a steep valley. Numerous holes showed where locals were still digging for bricks. We walked a bit further along to the end of a promontory above the joining of two valleys and had a panoramic view over loops in the river, the wheatlands in the valley, sheep grazing on the far hillsides and above the other side of the valley the mountain slopes going upwards showing signs of ancient terracing, and storage caves as ingenious as those I'd seen in Cappadocia. This was Sassanid ground. Their empire was one of the greatest in history, stretching from the Indus Valley west through Samarkand and Tashkent. King Shapur defeated Rome, forcing it to give up Mesopotamia and Armenia, and swept to power in Syria and Cappadocia. Shapur was a man of vision and interest in sciences. His court had a resident ambassador from China, and he settled thousands of defeated Roman legionaries in Persia to provide his empire with architects, engineers and technicians. Some of the Roman bridges and barrages are still in use in parts of Iran.

From the headland we followed the line of wall to where it turned right; it was here that the professional archaeologists had lost the trail and declared this to be the end of the wall. A little further east Elias pointed out where the next fort and castle had been, and showed me how the wall turned left running across a mountain-side. In his childhood the line of this stretch had been clearer, although it is still visible in autumn when the grass is dry. The line goes on deep into the mountains, down a fault in a near-vertical escarpment and on across a broad hilly plain. Elias pointed to the distant line, knowing its exact location.

We drove further along and intersected the wall again where it had crossed a river. The area is dotted with unexcavated burial mounds, virtually untouched by grave robbers because of the Turkoman belief that evil luck comes to anyone who desecrates a tomb. Thus they still lie intact with their bodies and treasures, and probably their households as well.

Perhaps the wall marches on to Mashhad, but we were overtaken by a dust storm and reluctantly turned for home.

4   A bath house with uncle

I had grown to love awakening at dawn out on the *talar*, and hearing all the horses slowly waking up and whinnying soft greetings as we washed and made coffee. And I adored my morning rides on the big white mare, those spacious horizons, and the scent of crushed sage under hoof.

But after a week I noticed that the river level was dropping. It would soon be totally dry. The wheat had ripened and I could hear its seed-heads clicking and rattling in the breeze, and the crack as the ears popped open. It was time to move pasture. We loaded all our gear, the saddlery, and some last sacks of vegetables for market into the jeep and left. Narcy teased me about their house in Tehran with its washing machine and cook. It was difficult to imagine him and Louise in a house, they had been such happy nomads.

There were many military road blocks because some trouble had flared up with insurgents in the mountains. Above the forest we re-crossed the Elburz Mountains, whose peaks you can still see from the main street in Tehran. The Firouz house is in the centre of the city with its own private shady garden, an old building with some of the comforts of life, but no bedsteads. Here, as before, we laid our sheets out on floor-pads.

During the Revolution when Louise and Narcy came back to Tehran they were arrested and put in prison. 'But that's nothing special,' Louise had said. 'Most people went to prison for a while.' Many people had also been killed. Louise was in solitary confinement for two weeks, which ended when she went on hunger strike. Narcy was jailed for two months. Louise came back to the house which had been sealed and was in chaos, with slogans like 'Death to America' scrawled in lipstick and excrement. One of the slogans, written in lipstick, has been left in place, as part of the decor.

One morning we wandered around the local antique shops. I especially liked the miniatures, in some the figures were

stepping out of the picture on to their paper surround. Whenever I went out of the house I had to put on my scarf and
mantau. It felt absurd to be dressing up as if for an English
winter, the blazing heat surprised me every time. We also went
to the bazaar which has an astonishing number of gold shops.
I wondered who keeps them in business, there were few
shoppers. Gaggles of merchants seemed to be selling to each
other.

Traffic in Tehran is maniacal. Men drive cars just like they
drive donkeys, leaving the thinking to the donkey. And since
donkeys are driven at maximum speed, so are their vehicles,
while traffic lights flash, all three lights at once, seeming more
for decoration than for traffic control.

One day in a carpet shop I got into conversation with a man
who spoke out frankly saying that the Iranian people made a
mistake over installing Khomeni, though he admitted that he
was among those who had wanted the Revolution. 'We all
wanted it to come; if only the Shah hadn't hidden the facts of
life from us.' Illogically, he added, 'It was wonderful when the
Shah was here.' This line about how great things were under
the Shah was one I heard many times as people were forgetting
their earlier hardships in the light of the present ones. But they
say there won't be another revolution, because Khomeni sends
all the troublemakers to be killed in the fight against Iraq.

As for women, the Shah's twin sister and his wife had
championed women's rights, and in the sixties they won eman-
cipation into a male-dominated society, with equal pay laws
following in the early seventies, but it's all rather irrelevant
since a working wife is still an insult to her husband.

During the previous Shah's time, the wearing of the *chadoor*
had been made illegal. The effect was as shattering for some
women as to insist that all western women walk down the high
street in a bikini.

Now of course the *chadoor* or *mantau* is compulsory. Actually
I don't think the women mind as much as their liberated sisters
would want them to. They quite enjoy wearing one as a means
of flirtation, sometimes wearing little underneath, and it gives
the plain girl the same start as the beauty. Their natures are
lovely; and kinder, more generous people would be hard to
find.

Being female meant I could associate freely with Iranian
women, and over the full course of my journey I talked with

an enormous number, whose background varied from local bus passengers to the wealthy upper class. Segregation of men and women applies in all spheres, even the beaches are segregated, and on the female beach the women still have to wear a *chadoor* or *mantau*. It would be terrifying to swim in such a garment. A wife cannot play tennis with her husband, unless the court is private and not overlooked by public buildings. Iranian women who resisted covering up risked having acid sprayed in their faces.

It was time for me to move on; my visa was half expired so I bought a ticket on the public bus to Kerman which is 1,000 kilometres south-east of Tehran. The route took me through Qom, the fanatical and militant religious centre where Khomeni lived before he moved to the capital. Mosques dominated the oasis town, their minarets standing out against the sunset, and their loudspeakers crackling into the pre-recorded call to prayer.

Twilight was combined with a fierce gusty wind blowing sand along in dense clouds that rocked and peppered the bus like a sand-blasting machine. Between gusts I could see we were crossing a salt desert. In fact this is part of the Dasht-e-Lut, a desert which stretches over roughly 200,000 square kilometres of central plateau basins.

There are various types of desert in Iran. In salt deserts the salt lakes are *namak*, the *dasht* is a well-compacted gravel type, and the more treacherous *kavir* is a salt and silt mix which produces an unstable slime under a salt crust. It is best to keep to the ancient tracks hardened across it by aeons of hoof-prints. Outside the bus a large white salt-pan stretched to the darkening horizon.

Despite our being at over 1,900 metres the evening was hot. I sat in a front seat beside a stout matron who corrected the way I wore my *mantau*. When darkness fell the bus stopped for passengers to eat supper, Ramazan was over for the day, then we raced on into the night. Dozing, I thought how lucky I was not to have been born a man living in such a desert, but then I realised that every man here would consider himself luckier than me, he would never want to be a woman.

I disembarked the next morning in Kerman feeling a little jaded after the fourteen-hour trip and was thankful that I'd been given the address of a young couple, Issa and Pari-sima Ameri, who welcomed me to stay. Later Issa had to go out on business and he put me in the care of an uncle who could show me the old parts of town. Kerman is described by Strabo as having a river which brings down gold dust; he noted mines of silver, copper and asbestos, and two particular mountains, one of which contained arsenic and the other salt.

We started at the bazaar. Kerman has been famous for its metal-craft since the Bronze Age. Whole alleyways of coppersmiths sat hammering busily, flattening copper dishes, punching holes in rice-steamers, making handles to fit. Furnaces were roaring as men smelted and wielded hammer on anvil.

Kerman's bazaar has four gates and it was formerly on such an active crossroads of trade routes that the bazaaris became specialists in the transit-trade for furs, silks, textiles, birds, cattle, fruit trees, and precious stones. Alexander the Great had a rendezvous here with some elephants. Later Marco Polo passed through Kerman on his outward journey to China in the thirteenth century. He noticed that the inhabitants excelled in making equipment for mounted warriors – bridles, saddles, spurs, swords, bows, quivers and every sort of armour.

The bazaar still has its ancient caravanserai and a 400-year-old *hamam*, or public bath house, which has been turned into a museum, with vaulted ceilings, tiled walls, Persian carpets and a marble-edged pond of goldfish. The *hamam* used to be open to men in the mornings and women in the afternoons. Some rooms had fire bowls to heat water for tiled bath tubs. There was a swimming pool with lion's head fountain, and a cold pool beside the massage area where patrons' skin was scrubbed with rough pads and blown on to through short pipes to help the circulation. Soap was made in cakes of goat's fat. Alcoves were set aside for haircutting, believed to prolong a boy's life, and marble tables for painting henna on fingers and toes. Another similar bath house in the bazaar is still in daily use. Uncle and I sat down for a glass of *baludeh*, the speciality drink of Kerman which looks like frog-spawn but is sweet and icy.

On the way home we passed a fort made of colossal baked mud bricks, and a *yaghdun* which was an ancient ice-making house. It was May and the weather was already sweltering hot, but uncle said in winter it was cold enough to make ice. The pyramid-shaped building contained a sunken pool where the ice formed, and room for ample blocks to be stacked. The ice supply could last well into the summer months. Nowadays there are ice-factories. Uncle chuckled then burst into a story in rapid Farsi, totally incomprehensible to me, though he kept slapping his knees and cackling with mirth. The sight made me begin laughing, it didn't seem to matter that I couldn't grasp the joke.

We reached Issa's house in time for lunch of chicken kebab, and for my siesta I lay on the floor watching John Wayne in a Farsi-dubbed cowboy film. When the afternoon heat grew less intense, Issa took me to see his horses stabled at a hamlet an hour's drive away.

On the town's outskirts attempts are being made to grow tamarisk, a dry earth shrub which can help turn desert into arable land, and is particularly useful in lessening the dust storms that used to plague Kerman. Another of Issa's uncles had pioneered this scheme, after studying desert reclamation in Israel. Now the tamarisk was mauve in flower.

Beyond it the desert opened around us, grey-black stony desert mountains looking like the shore of a prehistoric sea. Dustdevils spun thirty metres tall.

Reaching the hamlet I could see that it only existed because of Issa's horses, tended by local men and their families and watered by a one-hundred-metre well. With water so deep, and rather salty, villages are scarce. This well is sufficient for a bit of irrigation, primarily for lucerne and pistachio nut trees. Issa stopped to check their fruit and he pointed out how much more the low bushy trees yield than the tall ones. Herds of sheep were being milked. The ewes' udders are tied up in cloth bags during the day so that their weaned lambs cannot suckle. After the women have taken enough, the lambs have their turn.

The stables, a rambling domed mud-brick building of many interlinking rooms, contained a herd of about ten Arab mares and foals while the stallion was stabled separately. Issa brought him out on a lunge rein, a pure black Arab stallion, 15 h.h., very impressive as he stamped and snorted with eagerness to get at the mares. After serving two of them he was given half an hour's lunging, and his paces were a delight to watch, his trot sailing through the air, all four feet in the air more than on the ground; stretching his forelegs, tail and head high, a picture of vigour.

As I understand it, Arab horses did not originate in Arabia. Far back in time, Persia supplied Arabia with horses. In Persia the equine had evolved into various modern breeds with three main Arab groups: the Plateau Persian, Darashuri and Kurdish

Arabs. The British version of the Arab is the Anglo-Arab, where selective breeding has emphasised features like the dish face and flattened forehead. Among the Iranian herds one horse in ten may naturally have this flat forehead and overshot jaw, but it is labelled locally as a *goter puseh* (a mule with a flat nose) because when Arab mares are crossed with donkeys the mules often have that conformation. It is not esteemed since the flared nose makes its jaw fit badly and causes nasal breathing problems.

In Kerman the following morning, I was awoken at 5 a.m. by the smell of fresh hot bread, and after breakfast I went riding at another stables where the stable manager thought he would please me by lending me an imported Irish thoroughbred mare. Seventeen hands high, very docile, she moved as though her feet were tied together with a short string.

The stable manager, Tamoor, escorted me on a fine pure Turkoman mare, and we set out through a village and across the flat desert. At a series of small gulleys I set my horse into a canter to jump them. She jumped well, almost taking them in her stride, and as Tamoor's Turkoman came galloping past we began to race across the open flatness, crusty from recent rain, the dust puffing under our thudding hooves. The only vegetation was camel thorn and a very occasional desert flower.

After about half an hour Tamoor let me ride the Turkoman who was far more spirited than the stomping Irish mare, and wouldn't calm down to any leisurely pace. We reached the tall embankment of the trans-Iranian railway line which ends at Kerman, and Tamoor recommended we galloped to the top. The horses fought for their heads, I relaxed and let my mare choose her pace, charging up to the top without pausing. Then we walked along beside the tracks as Tamoor assured me that the daily train wasn't due until the afternoon.

Back at the stables I took a look at some of the other fifty horses, mostly Kurdish Arabs, and one of a very rare breed, the Clat. Clats were indigenous to northern Iran, but according to Tamoor the Russians took nearly all of them. This one, a bay stallion, was 16 h.h. of strong heavy build with the typical hook nose of the early steppe horses.

The wide range of indigenous breeds which evolved in Iran is due logically to the land; the drier the desert, the smaller and more finely built were the horses, while in the lush limestone hills they became big-boned and fleshy, the famous Nisean was

17 h.h. The importance of horses was that not only were they man's fastest transport for 4000 years, but they provided superiority in war; history would have taken a different course without warhorses.

Most of the horses in the stables wore an amulet or decorative neck-band, with a verse from the Koran to avert the evil eye.

As we drove back into town I noticed a strangely-dressed and ragged group of people who Issa said were Luli, a gypsy race who are plentiful around Kerman. Issa detoured on the way back to show me the Zoroastrian quarter of town. There are still numerous believers in this creed which sprang up circa 500 BC. Zoroastrians intermarry, so keeping themselves pure, and have a different Farsi dialect. They worship at a sacred fire and celebrate around Christmas, building wooden towers for a torchlight festival. We drove around the outskirts of Kerman where it backs up against dry mountainsides, through an old cemetery with an octagonal stone tomb and bracketed dome. Nearby are some Zoroastrian buildings that were used as offering places, where food was placed and a wish made, somewhat like the old Farsi custom of making offerings to the dead. Coming back we passed the tomb of Moshta Ghalishah, a Sufi dervish who was stoned to death for putting the Koran to music.

We had lunch with some of Issa's cousins. A big family, their daughters gave me a lesson in Persian dancing, disregarding the fact that this is illegal. Music is also banned, so we kept the volume low in case any of the neighbours reported us to the Revolutionary Guards. The dance was a hip-flicking, shoulder shaking effort, which made me feel stiff and inflexible. But as one of the daughters, a heavy lump of a girl, began dancing, she was transformed into a light-stepping image of gracefulness, dancing from feet to fingertips, swaying and shimmering as her shoulders flickered to and fro, both shoulders at once. She said it had taken her years of practice to learn that movement. It seemed a shame that to display such grace was now a crime.

5 Dancing Arabs and desert water

From Kerman I went by bus to Bam, only four and a half hours south-east away across a gravelly desert studded with pincushion shrubs in purple bloom. Flatness gave way to ripples of low hills bisected by gorges. Most other people on the bus were Baluchi, the semi-nomadic tribe whose territory covers much of south-east Iran and western Pakistan. The Baluchis' origins don't seem to be recorded, except for phrases like 'they have no ancient literature, are very ignorant and pride themselves on this ignorance.' Also as 'greedy, conceited, unwilling, and unreasonable as a camel. But they're honest, very moral, living up to their own code of honour, and they treat their women as equals.' Like other tribeswomen, these were not wearing the *chadoor*.

I wasn't worried about where to stay in Bam since it was Issa's parents' home and he had telephoned his father. A jeep was waiting to collect me from the bus stop. Issa had forewarned me to keep a low profile because Bam's three leading families were continually feuding, and as Mr Ameri was head of one of these families, Issa was anxious in case my presence triggered a new feud.

The jeep whisked me through a warren of narrow lanes between tall clay walls. We stopped outside iron gates and I walked into a courtyard, to be greeted by Issa's mother and father and refreshed with *dogh* (watered-down yoghurt with finely chopped herbs) and biscuits. Then Mr Ameri took me to see his stables, obviously his pride and joy. And with good reason, the airy domed mud stables held ten magnificent Arab stallions. Mr Ameri is renowned for his horses. 'Would you like to ride this afternoon? You can try out my best horse, he's a Dancing Arab.' Undaunted I accepted, hoping that its mouth and manners would be as good as its conformation.

On the other side of the walled street we visited the stables of Kooros, a cousin, who told me that their mares are kept 100 kilometres away in the desert and offered to take me there the next day.

We ate lunch sitting on a carpet with dishes spread on a floor cloth. The main dish was *kormehsabsie* (beans and beef), and *mast*, followed by dates which we also spread *mast* over. A good combination. During the meal Mr Ameri talked slowly and authoritatively, as befits the head of a family. His wife wore a headscarf and muslin *chadoor*, perhaps because Kooros was present. She looked too young to be the mother of five grown children, and now that they have all left home she said the house felt empty.

It's a roomy white-plastered house built around the four sides of a large courtyard, with a pond in the centre. From the rooftops rise several wind towers, multi-sided with tall hollow grooves to catch the wind from whichever direction it might blow and channel it down to the rooms beneath. In one of the wind towers the breeze is sent across a pool of water to cool and moisten it. That's what I call air-conditioning.

The domed ceilings one sees everywhere here are also a simple device for reducing the desert heat, on the principle that hot air rises and escapes through a hole at the top. Even the village huts and stables employ this principle, and indeed they are as cool inside as one could hope for in a desert.

When the afternoon heat passed we made ready to go riding. My *mantau* was hanging on a circular coat-stand outside my door and as I unhooked it I saw that a bird had built its nest in the coat-stand's branches, and laid three speckled brown eggs. Grooms rode the horses to the edge of town while we drove there and waited for them near the carcass of a dead donkey.

As the four stallions approached I could pick out the one I'd selected, already in a lather of sweat, jibbing sideways and looking a thoroughly difficult ride. Mr Ameri said he was called Sohail, which is the name of a star that shines between September and December.

Mounting him was tricky because he got in a fever of prancing, but I leapt aboard during a slight lull, and off we went. A dancing horse, yes, dancing in every direction, seeming incapable of straight lines, with a marvellous *pas-de-deux* of legs lifting high, but despite all this he was great fun. Not an ounce of vice, and light-mouthed, never really pulling, just playful. Closeness to other horses excited them all. Thank goodness we had the whole desert without obstructions, and we used it, spreading out over the grey gravelly ground in a line abreast and heading for distant mountains. I set Sohail into a canter and he leapt into a bounding motion flicking his back legs up. Yet even at that speed he moved further sideways than forwards, though so agile he never tripped.

The Dancing Arab horses of Isfahan are a type kept specifically for traditional religious plays, in which battles and manoeuvres have to be performed in a small arena. Rather like the Lippizaners in Vienna, these dancing horses can do *levades* and high flying changes.

We met up with the other riders from time to time. Mr Ameri rode in the style of the grand seigneur, while the groom slouched in the saddle like a sack of potatoes. After about seven kilometres we turned for home. I was cantering out ahead when I heard shouts and suddenly saw a riderless horse galloping across the desert towards me. Somehow I made Sohail behave sensibly and we caught the loose horse. Though once I had hold of its reins, I slid off Sohail's back; it would have been impossible to lead another stallion from his back. I returned the groom's horse to him, but Sohail refused to let me remount by prancing around in circles and jumping sideways, so Kooros dismounted and held Sohail's head for me, after which Kooros' horse wouldn't stand for him to remount. What a circus.

The sun set in a dark cumulus of storm clouds while we were still five kilometres from home. Darkness followed quickly and I was impressed by the way the horses never faltered or stumbled. Perhaps because they pick their feet up so high they simply don't trip over things like other horses. The cavalcade trotted, Sohail pranced; the men admire the way he dances, but I rather wished he'd relax.

Since it was dark no one minded me riding through town. We clattered along the narrow alleys, women scattered out of the way and pressed close to the walls, though we slowed so as not to frighten them. Bicycles came along without lights, but they could hear the horses and avoided us. Passing some orchards I could smell lime and orange trees in the evening stillness before a storm. The horses quickened their pace. Furtive opium-smokers darted into dark shadow. Dogs barked angrily. Lightning forks split the black sky. Finally I recognised that we were near home and the last few alleys were negotiated with ease. After handing Sohail over to his groom I went to Kooros' house which is set amid a date and grapefruit orchard, to relax with a long drink of iced water. But I'd got a terrible bout of hay fever and was sneezing myself silly. We went back to the Ameris' for a late supper and when Mr Ameri saw my plight he called for some *calpuray*.

I've never found anything that stops hay fever (except pills that make you too drowsy), and was intrigued by the arrival of a small bag of dried herbs. Just by sniffing it occasionally my sneezes abated. Kooros said that it's effective against all sorts of allergy.

At 4.30 the next morning Kooros collected me and we went to the old acropolis of Bam, which was built 2,000 years ago and lived in until early last century. The sky was streaked with dawn rays and I could just discern the bulk of the lower city's mud walls, with the upper city on the hill summit.

'My grandfather was born here,' said Kooros. 'Our family house was in the upper city. Come on, let's go to the top.' Narrow cobbled lanes twisted steeply up, with cobbles flattened and worn by the tread of men and beasts, the houses semi-ruined, though many still boasted ornate wind towers. In the broken walls I could see how buildings were constructed of baked mud bricks covered by a five-centimetre-thick layer of chopped straw and mud plaster.

We reached the citadel just as the sun rose above the desert. To the west lay the present-day city of Bam while below us lay the old outgrown one. 'Only the important families lived in this upper part, look at the size of this house.' It was more like a mud palace, still in almost perfect condition with a multitude of rooms leading from small courtyards. 'My grandfather had seventy-two wives; he said they kept him feeling young, and he proved it by living for 102 years. My great-great-grandfather was a Khan. His name was Hadj Mohammed Kerim Khan and he became Governor of Kerman and Baluchistan.'

At 5.30 a.m. the sun was already blazing hot. On the way down we stopped at a house in the lower city which has a room with a well in it. This room is still in use, there are oil lamps and pictures of holy Moslem men. Kooros explained that this is a shrine dedicated to Ali, the son-in-law of the Prophet whose death caused the split in Islam which resulted finally in the two rival sects of Sunnis and Shi'ites. The latter believe in the return of Ali and, according to Kooros, this well was a shrine associated with his return.

We breakfasted at the Ameri house, then set off by jeep into what was to be an extraordinarily interesting day. We were driving 120 kilometres south-east to see the Ameri mares. 'And I'll take you to my village,' Kooros began. 'When I bought my village I had to sell all my sheep and cattle to afford it. And I had to work desperately hard to pay the expenses of keeping the place going.'

'Why did you buy a village?' I asked. To me it seemed a curious purchase. But Kooros' answer was, to him, very simple.

'Because I haven't inherited any. My father is still alive. My grandfather owned fifty villages, which were bequeathed to my father, uncles and aunts in the normal Islamic ratio of two parts for the boys and one part for the girls; so that if thirty villages were to be inherited by one son and five daughters, the son would receive twenty villages and the daughters would have two each. If a village needs to be divided among many people, they can all have shares. A village can be owned by any number of people.' He pointed to an oasis of rectangular mud buildings with oblong domed roofs. 'That's Moradaba, it belongs to about twenty people; they share the costs and profits.'

'What are the costs and profits?' I interrupted.

'The owners have to pay for everything the villagers need: their building materials for new houses, their water supply, and their monthly wages. The profit comes from the crops; here they grow lucerne, wheat and fruit; and the harvest belongs to the village-owners, although they give a monthly supply of wheat to the villagers, and one third of the lucerne goes to the villagers for animal fodder. The majority of the crops and fruit belongs to the owner who takes what he needs for his family and his livestock, and sells the rest at market. But a lot of the money comes back into the village to cover those expenses I mentioned, and of course there's the cost of the *qanat*.'

'*Qanat*?' I queried.

'Yes, I'll show you my *qanat* when we get there, but you can see others both sides of this road, those lines of what look like bomb craters, they are many entrances to *qanat* tunnels.'

My eyes took in the crater mounds about fifty metres apart in regular lines across the flatness of sand; they shimmered in heat haze and the more distant mounds seemed to be floating as islands in a mirage.

The land outside was featureless except for the *qanat* mouths stretching back towards the foot of a mountain range. Iran is reputed to have over 50,000 *qanats*. These underground tunnels bring water from where it collects in the sand and rock below mountains, and by sloping the tunnels at exactly the right angle the water can be channelled as far as forty kilometres (the longest on record is seventy kilometres) under the desert, emerging in low-lying areas as streams to create an oasis. Or they can be reached via wells along the way, if there's enough water for more than one village.

The many entrances are useful for the removal of excavated and dredged sand in the tunnels. Also they provide some light and oxygen for the boys burrowing down there, and access during yearly maintenance. Roof-falls and partial collapses are not uncommon as the tunnels grow older. 'How many years does a *qanat* last?' I wondered aloud.

'A good one can last over 100 years,' Kooros replied, 'but sometimes the source will dry up, or become too salty.'

I told him how I had seen *qanats* in the desert of north-west China where they're called *karez*, and Kooros explained how the technology to build them had come from Iran several thousand years ago. In the Persian war, Alexander's army had destroyed towns by filling in their *qanats*. Then he sighed and apologised for his poor English. 'Talking English is hard, it's been twenty-four years since I last had a conversation in English!'

I was amazed that he could speak it so well. He had spent a year in America as a student, and although he had been shy about speaking when I first arrived in Bam, he was now trying and I was impressed by his effort. We lapsed into an amicable silence. I gave us a drink from the iced thermos, there's nothing to equal cold water in a desert. Further on we swung left down a barely defined track across the sands to Kooros' village. Dunes rose from the flatness and a man on a camel trotted past.

'This is my *qanat*, it's quite a new one, the deepest end is sixteen metres. That's a reasonable depth, they're sometimes 100 metres, and the deepest I've heard of is over 300 metres. It's expensive to build, and that's how many feuds get started, like when someone builds a well which draws from someone else's supply.

'In fact we have laws about the distance there must be between *qanats* and wells; and if two *qanats* run close together usually one is deep and angled gently, the other is higher and angled more steeply. The water in a *qanat* belongs to the man who built it. The land which a *qanat* waters becomes his also by right, and here this has always been so. If there's more than one *qanat*, the land is shared. And water rights can be sold, inherited and sub-divided.'

'What's that thing?' I asked pointing to a wooden pole frame over one of the mouths. 'It's a pulley for hauling the baskets of sand out. The *kahkin* (*qanat* boys) must be cleaning out the tunnel below.'

The mouth was four metres deep, the water looked cold and clear. Some of the mouths we looked at were covered by a slab of wood to prevent sand drifting down. At an open mouth we could hear the voices of two *kahkin* echoing along the tunnels. They called to each other with precise words, using the language they have evolved for communication in *qanats* where sound distorts. Theirs is a risky life, trying to free blockages, working in an underground river with a small pick and shovel.

From there we drove past various old fortified villages. One had a tall round watchtower with raised patterns in its mud walls. In general the fortified villages were very small and could not have housed the whole village on a permanent basis, but Kooros explained that each family kept one room inside for safety. 'In my grandfather's day the village owner also paid for his village's protection. These four villages here belong to Mr Ameri. I think he's got about seven in all.'

Sun blazed down; mirages of sea with lapping waves melted into illusory swamps. This is all part of the Lut Desert. A herd of camels was being shepherded by a Baluchi in green and gold turban. He recognised Kooros and waved a greeting. 'We're near the Ameri mares,' Kooros told me. 'Let's stop to see them.' We turned towards an oasis, bouncing roadless over the sand.

The eight mares were in a spacious corral; one was a top-grade International Arab and the others were Darashuri. The original Bam Arab horses were Saglavi, which is not an officially recognised breed since it's an untraceable bloodline.

There were no horses at Kooros' village, but he offered me a ride on his camel instead. The camel was rather stroppy about being saddled but knelt obediently for me to clamber on. The saddle was two bars and a pad and I sat back behind the hump. Unbridled, it had a nose peg and rope which worked just as well, and when the camel rose up I steered it into a tour of the oasis. Its pace was a swinging jog, far more comfortable than the camel I had owned in Africa which would only walk and even at that pace it had felt like riding in a ship's crow's nest during a storm. The faster pace of this camel and its comfortable saddle were great improvements.

In the village some girls were baking bread, slapping flat oblongs of dough into the sides of a clay oven; the girls offered me one they'd just peeled out of the oven but the camel wouldn't stop, its nose-rope had come adrift from the peg and we went careering away.

Since there was now no way to stop or steer it, I didn't worry, letting it take me past fields of henna in creamy flower. Henna dye would be obtained from the seeds that followed. Skirting the fields we entered a date-palm grove, the branches swept into me, I pushed them upwards minding out for the thorns, which was tricky, since the camel wouldn't slacken its fast pace and was doubtless trying to brush me off its back.

It was time for me to reassert control. Making a loop in the rope I managed to throw it over his nose-peg, and persuaded him to stop. Someone came over and attached it properly, and taught me the commands for stop and lie down – *kkkk*; and to go faster – *och, hake, ah-ping*, and various clicking noises.

An avenue of casuarina trees led me back to where Kooros was standing. 'Make room for me,' he called, 'and I'll show you the way to another place.'

He sat in front of me and we rode across the desert sands for a short way to a Baluchi encampment. Some of its huts were like elongated wigwams of poles covered in mud, others were tent-shaped with a ridge pole; the sides were made from dry palm leaves and I noticed people sprinkling water on them to cool the air inside.

The women around the camp wore brightly coloured dresses with full skirts. Small of stature, their height was built up by wearing a headpiece draped in scarves and shawls. One woman was carrying her baby, bound up like a papoose and its legs were tied straight.

On the way back the camel had to cross a stream. 'This is the water from my *qanat*,' Kooros announced proudly. His pride suffered a dunking since when the camel reached the stream it simply sat down in the water. Nothing would induce it to stand up, until both Kooros and I had slid off its back into the water.

Finally we walked back to Kooros' village leading the camel, and drank several glasses of *dogh* to quench our thirst. When we left his village Kooros drove a different route through the desert, pointing out villages belonging to his father and relatives. 'I lived in that one for eleven years before I was married, it's owned by my uncle and I worked there to organise its agriculture. A hard but happy life.'

Beyond some sand dunes four ruined towers were just visible and I asked Kooros if we might take a closer look. We found ourselves beside an ancient clay fortress. Its walls and corner towers were crumbling, and its gate-house barred by a tangle of sticks and poles.

'This was my grandfather's summer home,' Kooros said as we climbed between the poles and emerged into the courtyard. It was now being used as a camel stockade for female camels with young babies. The youngsters ran to hide behind their mothers' legs and peered out at us. Having not yet developed the supercilious stare of their elders, their long-lashed eyes were agog with curiosity.

'That blocked door was my room, on its left was my servant's room and that domed shady place on the right was the stables.' His matter-of-fact description brought vividly alive this place of memories and baby camels.

Back in Bam in the late afternoon we took the horses out for a twenty-kilometre ride. I rode a bay stallion, fiery and boisterous, and we went north-west along the plain, parallel to the mountains. It was dark long before we turned for home, and by the time we reached town I felt exhausted. The scent of citrus trees revived my senses and my body recovered after a cold shower and a drink of iced date juice. The juice is not made from the dates themselves but from the flower of the male tree.

At supper the bird which was nesting in the coat-stand tried to distract attention from its eggs, swooping into the room and perching on the electric light flex, making the bulb swing and sending patterns of light spinning around the walls.

I slept out in the courtyard for coolness and fell asleep watching galaxies of stars moving slowly across the night sky.

Three

BALUCHISTAN

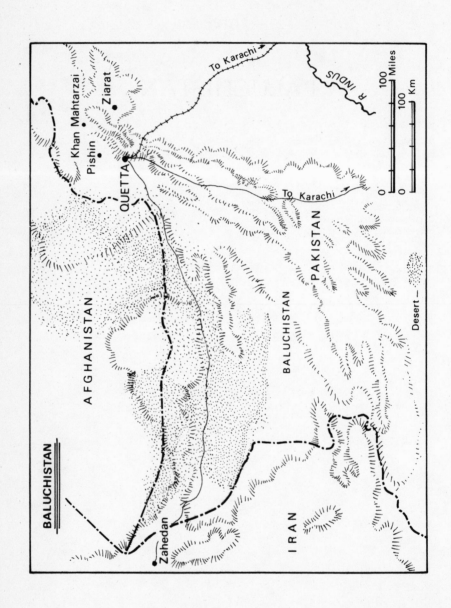

6   *Afghans and Zoroastrians*

My goodbyes had already been said and at 4 a.m. one of the housemen drove me down to catch the bus to Zahedan near the Pakistan border. My transit visa was expiring and I had to leave Iran, but I hoped to obtain a new visa in Karachi. From the bus I watched my third sunrise over the Lut Desert and tried to see the ancient lighthouse which once served much the same office as a coastal light, guiding caravans in from the desert. We drove through a region where acres of mud-rock cores stood up above the flatness, looking like a vast ruined city. In bygone days they had given rise to legends of lost cities.

They were followed by undulating grey desert cut by hidden valleys, with the occasional ruined fort. The bus stopped to pick up some Baluchi families, their womenfolk in colourful dresses and undertrousers with silk embroidery on the legs and sleeves; much smarter than everyday village clothes. All the men on the bus wore turbans.

Baluchistan is a huge but sparsely peopled desert country now divided between Iran and Pakistan; the whole of Baluchistan belonged to Persia around 500 BC but it was always an isolated and fiercely independent frontier state. The Persian empire had also included Karachi, capital of Sind. My journey would stay within that Persian empire, going no further east than Baluchistan and Sind.

At Zahedan I changed buses and reached the Iran – Pakistan frontier at 11.30 a.m., to be greeted by the information that the border was closing until 4 p.m. The sand was frying hot, I had to sit in the customs shed and didn't dare eat or drink since it was still Ramazan. What a relief it would be when the fast finished in a few days' time.

Out behind the customs shed I found a tap, but the water tasted salty. I had longings for cold fresh water, the air was very dusty and washing my face only brought temporary relief. But I mulled over the thought that salty water is probably a far healthier drink for desert dwellers than unsalted.

It was a tedious wait, I couldn't even write my diary for fear
of Iran's jitteriness. Slogans daubed on the customs yard walls
read 'All we want is the laws and rules of Islam all over the
world'. Another reads, for a change, 'Down with USSR'. And
the quarantine hall's entrance is marked 'England is worse than
America, and Russia is worse than the world'.

After the four-hour wait I crossed the border, entered Pakistan, and found a bus leaving for Quetta within the hour. I filled
the time looking for water, there didn't seem to be a public tap
anywhere in the scrawny town, not even a salt-water one. And
when I asked for a loo they said sorry there's only a loo on the
Iran side, here the people just squat in the desert. In contrast
to the clean Iranian towns, this place was squalid, filth and
faeces everywhere, stagnant grey ditches, piles of rubbish
picked through by goats and people, and most of the houses
were shanty shacks made from old packing cases and tin.
Everyone I met seemed to be a black-market money-changer.

The bus didn't leave after an hour, it didn't leave after two
hours, nor after ten. It just sat waiting for more passengers to
fill it. That blew my chance of getting across the longer half of
the desert by cool of night. After twelve hours I felt as exhausted
as I would have felt from travelling, or perhaps the effort of
travelling nowhere was harder. When the sun set and darkness
settled, we passengers lay down to sleep in the bus.

Dawn came, the heat started to intensify. The only cheerful
thing was the bus itself, gaudily decorated with shiny tin
cutouts, while the front was emblazoned like a shield with
multi-coloured glass reflectors. Dazzling in the sun, and buses
generally try to out-display each other.

Finally the engine started, but we drove round and round
the town for another hour looking for more passengers, until
every seat was taken. At last we set off across the desert, but
within half an hour the motor conked out; we had run out of
fuel. I felt slightly defeated. Surely in the twelve-hour wait the
driver could have found some fuel. So there we sat, waiting for
another bus to come and perhaps give us some fuel.

A pick-up truck passed and our driver went with it to look
for diesel. Two more hours elapsed before we were on the
move. We trundled for twenty kilometres then stopped because
two buses were leaning against each other and blocking the
track. One had a broken axle and had fallen, or been propped
against the other. We stopped and ropes were attached to our

bus so it could pull the broken one upright. And since we had by this time lent our jacks and tools, we stayed until their repairs were done. It was a blazing hot day in a flat empty glaring desert, but I was impressed by the way men automatically helped each other, and women gave their water to those who needed it more.

The next 150 kilometres of dirt road was very corrugated, then we reached moth-eaten tarmac. The passengers bounced and swayed over the bumps in the road; their synchronised lurching almost fitted the music on the bus cassette player and looked oddly like a dance.

Dusk brought a sandstorm; a Baluchi passed leading camels laden with bits of root for firewood; most of my fellow-passengers were Baluchi and Afghan, with only five Pakistani townies. I allied myself with their three married women. On every long bus journey I make an ally of some suitable person or couple. As a woman, it saves trouble.

The air was still hot when darkness fell, we stopped at an oasis for chili-hot supper, the journey stretched through the night, and rain in the mountains caused a flash flood that we drove through up to the axles. We certainly fared better than Alexander the Great when he got lost in these Baluchi deserts and a flash flood removed most of his royal baggage.

Alexander conquered as far as the Indus, and launched an expedition downriver. Here he was following in the steps of the Persian King Darius, who had not only sent boats down the Indus to the sea, but had sailed through to the Mediterranean by building a canal linking the Red Sea and the River Nile. We reached Quetta at 10 a.m., it was bazaar day and the roads were choked with a beeping muddle of buses, rickshaws, donkey-carts and camel-carts laden with bricks. The camels had bells and scarves tied to their knees.

Roadside stalls were selling glittery embroidery, tin trunks, metal tools and offering shoe repairs or barbering. A pelican stood at a street corner, I thought it was stuffed until it pecked my sandal. Its owner showed me some jars of yellow oil and explained that he made pelican oil as a medicinal cure-all.

Though I dawdled in the bazaar, my first priority was to renew my Iranian visa. So I bought a ticket on the afternoon train to Karachi. It took twenty hours, growing hotter by the kilometre post as the train stopped at each one while descending the mountain pass. This was a safety measure, and I was reassured to see frequent run-off tracks had been constructed to halt runaway trains.

In Karachi I stayed at a travellers' hostel in the bazaar quarter, and was lucky to have an airy four-bed dormitory to myself. Outside, the trees were decorated with flashing coloured lights ready to celebrate the end of Ramazan, though the blue sparks of the machinery to rotate the lights were more startling than the displays themselves.

I browsed through the markets outside the hostel, past a dentist selling 'Mighty Resin Teeth', and a herbalist with a hooded cobra from which he made medicine to cure impotence. My supper at a café had far too much chili in it so I tried pulling out all the red bits, but it was a losing battle.

In the morning I filed my application for a new Iranian visa, and managed to catch city buses everywhere, a necessity since taxis and rickshaws tend to quadruple their prices for foreigners. On the buses, women sit in a closed-off section at the front, a welcome bit of chauvinism as men stand packed in a steamy crush at the back. I sat next to a woman who was holding a jar of water with two long fish curled in it. While I was wondering if they were alive, the bus lurched around a corner and the woman dropped the jar, spilling the fish on to the bus floor. Pandemonium broke out as they wriggled around with people trying to catch or dodge them. One fish slithered out the door into the road and the bus had to stop while the woman collected it, washed it under a tap and refilled her jar.

I lunched at the Sind Club, the oldest club in Central Asia. It was as elegant and luxurious as its reputation and my host was a retired Bengal Lancer I had been put in touch with by friends. Brigadier Heski Baig was also a world renowned polo player who had been in part responsible for the advent of polo in England. We talked about horses in Pakistan, but the indigenous breed of Simdi stock sounds inferior to Iranian horses. Most of the good stock here is imported from Europe.

The next morning as I strolled out to find breakfast in the bazaar I saw two monkeys and a porcupine sitting beside a man who was doing a juggling act. But as soon as his concentration was established the monkeys began teasing the porcupine by grabbing his unprotected parts, and the juggler had to collapse his act to rescue the poor old porcupine.

Later I saw the same man talking to someone leading a large brown bear on a chain. They showed me their act, which was to persuade a small boy to put his neck in the bear's mouth. Actually I don't think the bear had enough teeth left to do any damage.

Living in the bazaar was something I enjoyed, being able to stroll out and dive into the back streets, getting hopelessly lost but never far from my door. My friends were a hat-maker, a scarf-seller who would invite me to listen to BBC World Service News and drink sweet milky tea, and a tomato-seller whose motives were more dubious.

It would be a week before my visa was ready for collection, so I decided to see more of Baluchistan and caught the train back up to Quetta. It was packed with people going to family get-togethers to celebrate the end of Ramazan. This four-day public holiday is one of the four Moslem Eids or festivals and the date people start celebrating depends on the sighting of the new moon. On the train I travelled in a women's purdah compartment. The most closed version of purdah clothing is the Quetta model, a cloth from head to ground, with webbing visor so the woman can see out, giving a shuttlecock effect. As soon as the train pulled out of stations some women disrobed. We shared our evening food; my neighbour bought me some tea but when I tried to re-pay her for it she searched her mind for English words then said, 'No rupee, I love you.' That's a nice way of saying 'You're welcome.' There was henna on the soles of her feet, the centre of her palms, and fingertips, and her earrings started from the top of her ears. Her only other words of English were 'yes', 'no', and 'son-of-a-bitch'. She was one of an Afghan family from Kabul who were going back for a month because the fighting was not currently in their area.

In Karachi I had been given the names of Sheila and Jahansoz who met me in Quetta. Sheila is a Scot married to Jahansoz who is a Zoroastrian Parsi, originally from Iran, whence many Zoroastrians fled to escape forcible conversion to Islam. The Zoroastrians of Quetta have an *agyari* or temple where the mother flame, brought from Iran, still burns and is tended daily by its priest. Sheila is not allowed into the temple, nor permitted to become a Zoroastrian since it is not a faith that admits converts. Their two daughters, however, being born into it, are accepted.

As none of us was fasting for Ramazan we had a delicious lunch, and in the afternoon Sheila took me by jeep to an Afghan refugee camp up near the Afghan border. She used to work as

a doctor with the UN Medical Corps until a spate of trouble
and kidnapping caused a ban to be put on travel, making it
impossible for her to visit the camps and do her field work.

There are still restrictions on travel. The previous year an
Australian couple were kidnapped by Baluchi bandits and held
from May to October. The restrictions forbid foreign residents
to go outside Quetta town unless they take an armed escort.
So we took an escort and drove out on a new tarmac road which
felt soft as it melted under the hot sun.

Through villages and apple orchards we went into a marvellous region where red mud hills eroded into alluvial patterns
were backed by stark grey mountain ranges. Beside the road
were mangy-looking wheatlands being cultivated by nomad
women in reds and shocking pinks. The nomads' tents were of
black cloth, low and hooked up on guy ropes resembling large
black spiders.

It took nearly two hours to cover seventy kilometres. First
we passed a depot that provides the refugees with rations of
wheat, flour, cooking oil, and wooden posts for house building.
The refugee village itself had almost doubled in size since Sheila
was last here. Now three kilometres long and the same wide,
it had been established for six years and become a thriving
community with roadside stalls full of fresh fruit and vegetables.
It was the first day of Eid for them. The Afghans claimed that
the desert air was so clear they saw the new moon last night.
In Quetta the moon had not yet been seen.

My strongest impression of the refugee village was that this
was no poverty-stricken place of hardship and suffering; the
children looked well-nourished and healthy. There were a surprising number of men around, and from those I spoke to I
gathered that they go into Afghanistan to fight for a period
then retire here to heal their wounds or recover their energy.

The depressing thing was to see a superb collection of mobile
medical units, including a mobile X-ray unit and operating
theatre, being employed merely as overflow wards for lack of
Pakistani expertise in making use of them. What a waste of
foreign aid.

As Sheila and I drove back towards Quetta we went through
a herd of about 500 one-humped camels shedding their winter
coats. It occurred to me that this is the grazing land of a local
tribe, and I wondered how much they resent having their scanty
grazing gobbled by refugee camels. I had already heard about

local jealousy because refugees have free food and building materials, whilst the wells that are built for them on aid programmes are taking up precious locally needed water. It seemed unfair to me that the villagers who have the tribal right to scratch their living here should receive nothing while so much is being given away. There's always more than one side to any problem.

Quetta's vacant land has also become crowded with nomad tents, shabby patchwork shelters of Baluchis, Afghans and Pathans. Some Afghan girls told me they don't migrate into Afghanistan any longer. At a Pathan tent where I was invited for tea, a man played two flutes both at once, held apart at the ends so their beadwork fringes showed to advantage, and clasped together at the mouthpieces. Their sound was oddly like bagpipes and very melodious.

A dust storm blew up as I left. This town has such frequent dust storms I wonder why it doesn't follow the example of Kerman where Issa's uncle had beaten the elements by planting tamarisk.

Arriving back at my hotel at sunset, volleys of fireworks were exploding, perhaps to stimulate the appearance of the moon. As there was a power cut, I took a candle to my room and was reminded of the fireworks and candles in the Greek Orthodox Easter ceremony at the start of my journey. It had only been about six weeks ago, but somehow the time seemed to contain worlds travelled.

7 The Eid

The new moon had just been sighted and all night I heard firecrackers and the wailing of flutes. In the morning men were coming out of mosques, with much back-slapping and embracing. Children were paraded in full finery, and street vendors were open for business selling food and drinks. There was such an air of celebration that suddenly I felt forlorn and lonely. I wanted to see how the Eid was celebrated in the countryside and set out by local bus to the village of Pishin where there was to be a dancing and wrestling festival. But when I arrived there was no Eid festival – the mullahs had cancelled it – and no one could speak English. A helpful policeman led me to the house of an English-speaker and abandoned me at the gate.

The door was opened by an elderly Irish lady wearing ordinary Pakistani *salvar* and *kamise* (long shirt and baggy trousers), and this was how I came to meet the famous and respected Jennifer Qazi Musa, widow of Qazi Musa who had been partner to the founding father of Pakistan, Jinnah. Jennifer showed me the rooms that Jinnah and his wife had occupied during a visit and the whole house seemed to breathe a former age, decorated with swords, tiger skins, stuffed animal heads, and fading black and white photographs of the leading politicians of Partition days.

Local people tell the story that Jennifer had been given to her husband as a gift from King George VI of England because he had killed a lion. She refused to disillusion them.

Still in pursuit of an Eid festival, I changed direction towards Ziarat, a town in the mountains about 150 kilometres from Quetta. A bus took me thirty kilometres and dropped me at the side road to Ziarat where I was told there would be no more buses because the drivers were on holiday. No problem, I thought, I would hitch. But there was barely any traffic as everyone was at home feasting. Eventually a Range Rover stopped for me. The family were going beyond Ziarat to a government station where the husband who was a politician had business. He spent the journey lamenting the inadequacies of the regime, though he had a word of praise for the current Governor of Baluchistan, General Musa. 'He is a good man. In fact he is due to attend a village Eid in these parts today.'

'Where is the festival?' I pricked up my ears.

'At Khan Mahtarzai, fifteen kilometres off this road, we'll pass the turning in a moment.'

'Then that's where I'm going.' The mullahs couldn't cancel this celebration if the Governor was going to be present.

'If you insist, but be careful. This is a wild part of the world.' He let me out at the turning, I waved goodbye and when the Range Rover had vanished over the horizon I found myself alone in a gloriously huge empty landscape.

Three hours later I reached Khan Mahtarzai (good timing, the Governor was due to arrive within half an hour), and in the meantime I wandered through the throng. They were Pashtoon tribesmen wearing baggy pantaloons and shirts, their faces tanned and lean below turbans, fezzes or fur hats. Many of them had green eyes. Most men carried ancient rifles – and there were several thousand of them, no other foreigners, and not a single woman. It was quite a realisation to be one woman so outnumbered. On the high ground, where the village backed up against the mountain, men had already begun warming up their rifles, firing at distant targets. Below the village the grassy plain stretched to a far mountain horizon. The setting for the festival was a levelled area to one side of the village, with a canopy that shaded rows of chairs for the Governor and his entourage.

General Musa's arrival was heralded by sirens, militia and much firing of rifles by tribesmen. The official party and fifty of the *malik* (village dignitaries) took their seats under the canopy, and the Governor was presented with an ornate turban, or *kula*, traditional of this region. A young man stepped forward and sang some verses from the Koran, and the festival began with the ancient wrestling art of *kushati*.

Pairs of men bent over to lock shoulders and grasp each other's belts, kicking their feet forward at the same time to try and trip their opponent. One fall would decide, and the winners would compete until only one remained. It was a fierce display of skill and strength. The couple I enjoyed most were two white-haired old men who moved with grace and speed. The smaller man managed to hook his ankle around his opponent's leg and kept the position even though his opponent lifted him into the air. The crowd roared their approval. I had a good view of the performance because the official guard had given me a front row seat under the canopy.

For the competition of rifle marksmanship I walked over to the firing line. An armed soldier was sent as my escort, and was assigned to me for the rest of the festival. I admired the men's rifles, some very old with beautifully inlaid silverwork. Their aim over a hundred metres was surprisingly accurate, few of them missing the targets, though a bullseye decided the winner, shot by a tall handsome man in a wolf-fur hat.

Down on the levelled area a tug-of-war got under way, popularly won by the home team, and this was followed by dancing, a full ring of men with a drummer inside their circle, beating a cylindrical drum with sticks at both ends. Each village had its own dance group, some whirled and made circles within circles, spinning in opposite directions, the drum beat pounded and the atmosphere became a fog of dust.

At the end of the festival we were offered tea and cakes with fluorescent green and pink icing. The Governor called me over to be introduced, and I was also introduced to the village leaders. When I explained that I was on my way to Ziarat, General Musa suggested that I stay until the following day, and he asked the festival's organiser, Aziz, to make sure I was well looked after.

Aziz took me home with him to a hamlet a few miles away, and en route he explained how he had hit upon the scheme to organise the festival and invite the Governor in the hope that it would attract attention to the region. From what I had already gathered this area is poor and underdeveloped, although the land could yield plenty of crops if the government would invest some money into its development. For ten years Aziz had been requesting electric powerlines, and thanks to his perseverance, a supply had been connected the previous month. He offered to show me his orchards in the morning, but now it was time for the Eid feast – mutton, yoghurt, aubergine, cucumber, tomato and chapatis – and after the meal we sat back and sipped tea with sheep's milk.

Aziz's family was a delightful crowd of six young daughters. Their mother wore her yashmak aside, but when a male cousin came in, she quickly covered up and didn't even speak while he was there. At bedtime everyone lay on the floor of that main room, using carpets and quilts; it was almost chilly at this 2,800-metre altitude.

We awoke to a hot dawn, demolished a breakfast of eggs, sheep's butter, chapatis and tea, then I went to watch the women making the day's fresh supply of chapatis. A brushwood fire was kindled under the dome of a metal dish, and after kneading the dough the women flipped it skilfully between their hands until it stretched to a half metre in diameter, before laying it to cook on the hot dome. Buckets, ingeniously made from old truck tyres opened out and stitched into an urn-shape, stood by full of water.

'Come and see our well,' Aziz called proudly. His pride was because it symbolised his own investment in his land. It was over thirty metres deep, and in order to excavate it the diggers had created a secondary tunnel which sloped up to the surface. 'You can walk down it to the bottom,' he suggested, which I did and found the air deliciously cold.

Back on ground level Aziz took me to see his orchards, neatly laid out and irrigated. He grows peaches, apricots and four types of apples, also lucerne to feed his eighty sheep in winter when a metre of snow covers the land.

An enterprising man, I would write to the Governor saying how I had appreciated Aziz's hospitality and praising his efforts to cultivate the land. Aziz accompanied me to the Ziarat road and flagged down a jeep. It was already full of people but they were Aziz's friends and they moved over to make room for me.

The road descended and followed the base of a tall escarpment. The strata in the cliffs and hills made patterns of colour and texture: sharp grey, rounded black and smooth green, each eroding in a different way. As we approached the pass at 2,900 metres I began noticing juniper trees, for which the Ziarat region is famous. It has the largest juniper forest in the world. Over the pass the trees became more numerous, though too stunted and patchy to be called a forest, but Ziarat was still an hour distant along a rutted bouncy road among vast uplifts of sharp grey rock and vertically cut gorges. Gnarled trees hung from crevices making angular silhouettes.

We stopped in a valley to buy bags of black cherries and ate them sitting by a stream. An Afghan family arrived to fill some goatskins with water. The young girls were wearing high-waisted dresses of typical Afghan green and red with richly embroidered bodices. The mirror insets in the embroidery flashed sunlight from the sky and water, and the girls smiled without shyness.

In Ziarat I left the jeep and went for a long hike through the juniper forest. Some of the trees are said to be 5,000 years old. The end of my walk brought me to a spring of cold mountain water, where people were enjoying holiday picnics. Someone extolled for me the multiple uses of juniper. The pea-sized green fruit can be boiled to jelly and made into a poultice to speed the healing of broken bones; the old leaves make good fertiliser; the green leaves are excellent kindling and will burn even when wet; and the bark is effective as roofing to protect houses against cold and rain; it makes the house smell good at the same time.

Back in Ziarat's main square I had a 4 p.m. lunch at a café and watched a traditional Eid game of egg-breaking. It's generally played by children, dropping one hard boiled egg on to another in turn until one breaks. The winner takes both. Men were assembling for a wrestling contest. But soon after the wrestling began, the mullah ordered them all to go to the mosque and say prayers.

A truck gave me a lift back to Quetta and now it was time to go and see if my visa was ready in Karachi. I caught a minibus along a recently opened road. Purple rock and oleander bushes covered in pink flowers made it one of the prettiest desert routes I had ridden along. In Karachi my generous friend Brigadier Heski Baig showed me the polo stables and the rest of the day I spent doing my Christmas shopping in the bazaar and packed up the parcel to take to the Post Office. (I hate Christmas shopping in London in winter.) Parcels have to be sewn up in white cloth, and in the street outside the Post Office numerous people make a living at this. Seams have to be sealed with wax and stamped. Other men sit working on typewriters, filling in forms and writing letters for the illiterate. In the mêlée of rush hour traffic I noticed a policeman standing on a rostrum directing traffic with a huge smile on his face, his hand signals like those of a maestro conducting an orchestra.

From Karachi my journey led back through Quetta and west towards Iran on a bus trip that was nightmarish.

Four

PERSEPOLIS TO KURDISTAN

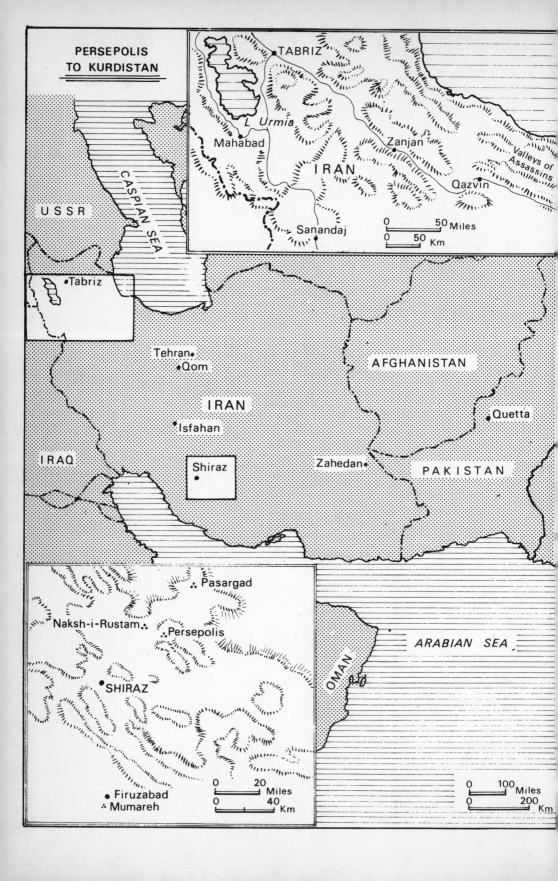

PERSEPOLIS
TO KURDISTAN

TABRIZ

L. Urmia

Mahabad

Zanjan

IRAN

Valleys of
Assassins

Qazvin

Sanandaj

0   50 Miles
0   50 Km

USSR

CASPIAN SEA

Tabriz

Tehran
Qom

IRAN

AFGHANISTAN

Isfahan

Quetta

IRAQ

Shiraz

Zahedan

PAKISTAN

ARABIAN SEA

Pasargad

Naksh-i-Rustam

Persepolis

SHIRAZ

OMAN

Firuzabad
Mumareh

0   20 Miles
0   40 Km

0   100 Miles
0   200 Km

8   In the footsteps of Cyrus

Having bought my ticket early, I thought it reserved a front seat and I went off for tea; by the time I realised it hadn't the choice had gone leaving only a seat at the very back. Unwise for a seventeen-hour bus ride on bad roads. The back bounced violently; how can anyone sleep through jolts that throw one's body into the air? Whenever I dozed off I whacked my forehead on the window bar. While the loudspeaker above my seat ensured I took the full blast of nasal Pakistani pop. It all made me feel a bit desperate.

Hot dusty air was pouring in through the open back door. Outside was featureless, not even a nomad in sight, nothing living or growing.

We reached the Iran frontier as it opened in the morning; I got through quickly and took a bus to Zahedan. In that short bit of road there were six road blocks for security checks. I noticed the weather seemed a great deal hotter than when I was here ten days ago.

From Zahedan I caught a bus going west to Shiraz and was impressed by Iran's better roads, newer buses with more legroom, and flasks of iced water. I lay back comfortably and watched a dust spout whirl outside, its funnel was spinning fast but without moving forward; it must have been ten metres in diameter and over thirty metres tall.

Grey lunar mountains rose from flatness. We stopped twice at security roadblocks where all the male passengers had to submit to body-searches. The soldiers didn't try to touch the women. My luggage was opened but no one was interested in the contents. The only thing worrying me was that I was wearing a long skirt to hide the fact that I wasn't wearing socks (too hot), and it was impossible to step back up into the bus without showing a leg. It may seem ridiculous, but I knew it was enough to land me in prison.

At the second roadblock we women didn't bother to get off the bus. I had a row of seats to myself so at dusk I stretched out and slept soundly for the first time in three nights. But sadly, the bus broke down at 4 a.m., in the desert, about 350 kilometres from Shiraz.

When another bus came along most people trooped aboard, standing room only. But I noticed an almost empty bus behind it and went to flag that one down. The full bus took off, and the one behind it didn't stop. That left me with two Baluchi tribesmen, and as dawn crept over the mountains we set off walking along the road. Little traffic came and nothing stopped. I wondered if they thought me an immoral infidel. Conversationally I asked my companions if they liked the Ayatollah Khomeni, and the vehemence of their reply surprised me. They made throat-slitting gestures and spat on the ground with disgust.

Eventually we got a lift in the back of a pick-up truck which took us along the shore of a large salt lake gleaming with crystalline whiteness. Its opposite shoreline of mountains and headlands stood out darkly. To the south the hills were clothed in fig trees. After fifty kilometres the two Baluchis said they were afraid of the driver's speed, and they left us in a town. I found a speed of 130-140 kph exhilarating so stayed in the truck.

We stopped at a roadside abattoir where the driver picked out a live goat and we waited while it was killed, skinned and gutted. Another man was cleaning three fat-tailed sheep's carcasses and I noticed how their fat tails are more like back-flaps of solid fat which is loved for its flavour. Our skinned goat, complete with head and eyes, was put in a polythene sack and dumped in the pick-up alongside my backpack.

I had come to Shiraz to see Persepolis and Pasargad, the two ancient capitals of Persia which lie only about fifty kilometres apart. My only confusion in asking directions was at a bus stop where someone told me to go to the police. 'No, no,' I said most definitely, but edged with desperation. Finally I realised he had said 'Perse-polis!'

However, I went to Pasargad first, being the earlier kingdom. Arriving there I felt slightly disappointed; little remains of Cyrus' palace except a few pillars of white marble on black bases. His only personal monument is a stone portrait on a slab of rock but the top half is missing. His tunic had once been inset with gold buttons, though the holes are now picked clean. The opposite side of the slab-style gateway has the bottom halves of a god with horse's feet and another with fishtail and legs.

In the jumble of fallen pillars and stone masonry I sat down to rest, it was midday and very hot, and I thought of mad dogs and Englishmen. I picked up a small rock and saw chiselled on the rock underneath it a beautiful miniature relief of a galloping horse and rider, with a Sassanian inscription.

Water channels, now dry, lead away from the palace and further away one can see they were formerly covered by street paving. There had also been irrigation for gardens that created the idea of earthly paradise. The word *par-di-son* in Farsi means a large garden. Pasargad's current remains are scattered over a wide area of bleached arid wasteland with a remarkable variety of thorny ground-plants, some in flower.

About half a kilometre away is a ruin with larger pillars than Cyrus' palace, one of them standing ten metres high; this was the Audience Hall, and on a square column I found an inscription which was translated for me by a one-armed man who had appeared from nowhere; he also showed me some Arabic inscriptions, and how the vast blocks of masonry were pinned together with big metal staples, a technique mastered by Cyrus' ancestors. Further north is a wall of a fire temple, and a solitary stone remaining from a fallen palace. Its carving depicts a winged man (Taj Mesra) from whose head grows a flame-shaped outline. Several kilometres further on are two stepped pyramid fire altars.

Cyrus' tomb stands alone, a square squat gabled edifice of cyclopean stone blocks, but not an ostentatious building. I managed to scramble up the blocks and ducked in through the low entrance – just tall enough to stand in with a smoke-blackened ceiling from people sheltering here over the millennia. At one side are carved motifs and an inscription which reads 'I am Cyrus, son of Cambyses, who founded the Empire of Persia, and was King of Asia. Grudge me not therefore this monument.'

The odd thing is that the monument is not impressive and, except for the size of the blocks, it represents extreme simplicity. This made me curious. None of the descriptions I had read seemed to have wondered if this tomb wasn't originally set inside an ornate exterior. And when I did some research I discovered that pillar bases of a superstructure had been noted around the tomb's exterior. This made more sense for the tomb of such a brilliant and powerful ruler as Cyrus. Near this site in 559 BC Cyrus' army overthrew the Medes. He went on to beat the Lydians with a new tactical weapon. As the Persian infantry advanced, led by bowmen in flowing saffron robes, they looked doomed, facing the long spears of the Lydian cavalry. But at the vital moment the Persian ranks parted and out galloped Cyrus' camels. Terrified by the unfamiliar sight and smell, the Lydian horses simply turned and fled.

These victories expanded Cyrus' kingdom by 3,000 kilometres and his successful administration made safe the trans-Asian caravan route which brought levies and taxes into his treasury. Not that Cyrus needed the money, he was already as rich as Croesus, literally, because Croesus was king of the Lydians and his treasure trove was stored in a fortress that Cyrus had conquered. Cyrus used the wealth wisely to build up and run his new empire, which would soon be the largest the world had known.

The construction of Pasargad incorporated Lydian ideas of architectural improvement; Lydian stone masons were brought to build the city, some came from as far as Ephesus on the Aegean coast, where they had to break off from building one of the seven wonders of the world, the temple of Artemis. Cyrus encouraged them to let their traditional style fuse harmoniously into Persian ancestral architecture.

After Pasargad was built, Cyrus invaded Babylon, freed the Jews and restored their temple in Jerusalem. He was killed in 529 BC by the Scythian Queen Tomyris who is said to have warned him, 'Rule your own people and try to bear the sight of me ruling mine.' But Cyrus forced a battle on her. She cut off his head in revenge for her son's death and threw it into a bag of human blood. His body was entombed here where I sat.

Now no bases of any superstructure are to be seen, particularly since the Shah had all around the tomb asphalted in 1970 for the festival celebrating 2,500 years of the world's oldest monarchy. But now the asphalt is invisible beneath weeds and thorny plants.

From the tomb I could see where the Royal Road, which had linked the Aegean across 3,000 kilometres to Asia, passed through Pasargad on its way to Persepolis. Beyond the tomb it entered a narrow gorge. So I set off to follow it.

Leaving that rocky defile, a good track follows a stream, the Pulvar river, which opens on to a large fertile plain, once called the Plain of the Water Bird. It is a beautiful plain, at a height of 2,100 metres, and edged by mountains that contain many natural caves. Some have mud walls across the mouth for stock holding. Villages are numerous, the buildings of mud and straw having rounded archways, and walls topped by a preserving overlap of bushy twigs covered in mud. In one village I bought a bag of dried cheese balls which smelt and tasted strongly of goat. Another clue were the goat's hairs firmly embedded in the dry cheese. I couldn't pull them out but munched them all the same.

9   Riding to Persepolis

The Royal Road from Sardis to Susa (which branched to Perse-polis) had post stations at intervals of one day's ride. Royal messages, with changes of horse and rider, could cover 2,500 kilometres in a week. Fragments of stone-paved surface are still visible near Bibahan but in this stretch my route relied on an ancient map and local advice.

When I met some village boys with horses I asked if I could hire one to ride to Naksh-i-Rustam and on to Persepolis. The idea proved acceptable and they squabbled over whose horse would earn the money. I interrupted and chose a leggy straw-berry roan, whereupon the youngest boy, a ten-year-old, as-sured me the horse was his responsibility and he handled our negotiations with practised shrewdness. After fitting my saddlebags on its back I mounted and tried to set out but the horse didn't want to leave and my urging made him buck. Determined not to fall off I clamped my knees to the saddle, and let him buck his fill as we cantered. At least we were moving forward and the bucking wasn't the jack-knifing kind of a bronco.

As our road led away from the greenness into an arid stretch, the horse calmed down and settled into an easy lope. I was just beginning to relax when I heard galloping hooves behind me and saw a loose horse following us, pursued by four boys on two other horses. Without too much fuss they recaptured the loose horse and one of the boys led it home. The others decided to accompany me for a while.

The land became more fertile again and the track led through wheatfields and across a main road. At midday I turned west along a path beside a stream. Its greenness of reeds and waterweeds was cool to my eyes.

One of the boys brought his horse alongside mine but there wasn't room for us both on the path, my horse was pushed on to the edge of the stream cliff, so I reined in. Soon the other boy was jostling me so I kicked my horse into a canter and outpaced them. But this didn't last, the boys were continually nudging me, though when I yelled at them they behaved better.

We forded that stream, then through a second stream, wading it where a small barrage had formed a shallow pool. The far bank was a steep scramble and I kept well to the side of my plunging horse. A small gallant one, its mottled red coat was soon generously splashed with mud and water. The three boys were riding two horses, and the smallest boy who had rented me my horse kept asking if he could ride pillion behind me, to which I said no.

At 1 p.m. we stopped by the stream to let the horses rest. I sat watching an enamel-blue kingfisher diving in the water; the boys sat too close to me for comfort, then pulled out a long knife and tried to frighten me.

But I had just begun a bout of hay fever and I couldn't pay attention to anything while sneezing almost continuously. The sneezing kept the boys at bay. And when it seemed to subside I walked over to my horse and secretly rubbed some of his dust under my nose. That produced another paroxysm of sneezes, and the boys eventually decided to saddle up again, though not without a final argument, in which the youngest boy ranged on my side and I said he could ride pillion with me if he made the other boys and their horses go home.

So the youngster vaulted up on to my horse's back behind the saddle, and yelled abuse at the older boys until they left. We loped away in the opposite direction, with my young ally sitting behind me easily on the horse's rump. The boys' behaviour wasn't out of character if one considers that many of the heroes and warriors of ancient Persia were bandits and robbers, which was not a disreputable profession. Travellers took such risks carrying money that, by the ninth century, credit notes and cheques were introduced. Our word cheque is of Persian origin.

We crossed another small river and came on to a plain where nomads had set up their black goats'-hair tents in the stony golden sand. Behind them a line of tall cliffs rose and sagged. The boy pointed to the end tip of the cliffs and shouted, 'Naksh-i-Rustam.'

I urged the horse into a canter, which the boy hadn't been expecting, and he nearly fell off backwards.

*   *   *

My pillion passenger was not giving much trouble, although he had again brought out the knife and waved it around until I told him to put it away. It was easy to get my revenge on him by making the horse trot, a most uncomfortable pace if you're sitting on its rump, and the boy soon learned to do as I said.

Approaching Naksh-i-Rustam, we could see bold cross-shaped tombs cut into the cliffs. These are the royal tombs of Darius, who followed Cyrus in an even more brilliant way; of Xerxes, intoxicated with power, who succeeded him; of Artaxerxes, a mild man who made a peace pact with Greece; and Darius II, the last in the weakening line. These were the Achaemenians, the first Persians. The tombs' cliff-face entrances are set high in rock polished and sculpted to show kings being respected by their peoples and blessed by their gods.

This point in the cliffs had previously been a sacred place of the Elamites, and later of the Parthians and Sassanians. The latter, whom I'd encountered civilised in north-east Iran, had here recorded their central power with great stone-carved pictures on panels of polished rock.

These magnificent panels portray men jousting on horseback, tilting with lances, and wearing thick robes and pointed helmets. One huge panel (10 metres by 5 metres) shows King Shapur receiving homage from a cringing Roman Emperor Valerian, who was captured in AD 260. Other relief panels depict royal investitures, triumphs, and the king surrounded by court finery. When I rode closer to them I could see how some are far more weather-worn than others, representing the rock art of over twenty centuries.

There are yet more panels further along the rocky bluff: two figures on horseback, one a god handing a crown to a king, who has a curious hair-bubble atop his head, while the god wears long curly hair and a crown. Their horses are trampling their enemies, the god's tramples Ahriman, synonymous with the forces of darkness. One should be able to identify the kings by matching their distinctive crowns to their coinage. As we rode past a carving of jousting my horse suddenly reared up. The boy slid off the back. Luckily only his pride was wounded, so I gave him my camera and asked him to take some pictures, which made him very happy. Grandiose stuff, the static dignity of the eastern heraldic style, but it doesn't have much artistic merit. Early Sassanian groups are set in single-file with the king the tallest man present. During Shapur's reign the artists introduced a new way of moulding drapery, learning from the Roman style of decorative relief how to make stone clothes on a curved body, and to compose scenes with groups.

The purpose of some panels seems to be a show of might to deter any further challenges, as at Bisitun where, in gory detail, nineteen rebellions are being squashed. Not artistic, but it doesn't lack effect. This was a vast and rich empire; the friezes weren't an understatement.

A square white marble building stands in front of the tombs, its base nearly six metres below ground level, an excavated trench showing a three-tiered plinth and a broken flight of marble steps. A water channel had run around the base. The windows are black marble and blind, unseeing, though the door is open, but the steps to reach it are missing. There has been much debate over the purpose of this building, though to me it looked like a fire temple. The fire-worshipping cult of Manes had been given official status by Shapur because the religion was a unifying factor within his empire and it supported the state's struggle against Christian Rome. This building would have been an ideal repository for sacred fire, kept alight by a priest, with blind windows so that no draught would kill the flame.

Around the bluff, invisible from the tombs, are two small fire altars, square with raised rounded corners, standing as tall as myself, so I had to climb the mountain slope behind to see down into them where the fire bowls lay empty. While on the hillside I found two sets of what seemed to be water channels, cut with deep sheer sides and spreading into a handful of channels. The only explanation I could think of was that they were channels for the blood of the animal sacrifices recorded by Xenophon.

From there I rode back on to the course of the Royal Road, following it along the base of the cliffs to a nomad camp. Some Qashgai girls were shepherding sheep, their faces rounded with high cheekbones, their hair growing low over the forehead, parted centrally and pulled forward in bangs threaded under red and pink tinsel-woven scarves. Their multi-skirted dresses were fluorescent colours with gold and silver embroidery.

A man on a white donkey galloped past, I was amused by the way its ears flapped as it ran. Another man rode by on a motorbike carrying a protesting goat with one hand, by the scruff of its neck. I reached down into my saddlebags and found the smelly cheese balls. The boy and I munched a few, he thought they were delicious.

About three kilometres from Naksh-i-Rustam where the valley narrows between craggy ranges we passed through the site of a ruined town. It would have been easy to miss, marked only by one pillar with a double capital of bulls' heads. But nearby are many pillars fallen from sight, and the foundations of buildings that had stretched extensively. There is also the more modern ruin of a caravanserai with fragments of one big mud wall still standing.

We rode on around the base of the eastern mountain range, crossing the stubble of harvested wheatfields where herds of sheep and goats were guzzling any fallen grain.

To cut across an unharvested field, my horse walked in a dry irrigation ditch. From that level the wheat was taller than the horse, and mixed with wild hollyhocks, blue-ball flowers and giant purple thistles. We crossed a river on a rickety iron bridge, below which men were picnicking and swimming in two pools. I pulled my headscarf forward so they couldn't tell I wasn't just a local woman.

We passed Naksh-i-Rajab, the site of more rock engravings. Plots of gold wheat were interspersed with green lucerne and sugar beet. I put the horse into a canter aiming to jump the next irrigation ditch. The boy held on tight, I had forgotten he was there.

Over two earthen ridges, we came down on to an asphalt road along the base of another mountain ridge. A brush-fire filled the air with clouds of smoke, but when the wind blew the smoke aside I could see in the very far distance the raised columns of Persepolis. My heart soared.

For the last stretch I cut back to the road, now a wide asphalt drive broad enough for six lanes. Being empty, I rode down the middle, and from an ambling trot the horse broke into a gallop. I would not normally gallop on tarmac, it's too jarring for a horse's legs, but the boy was whooping encouragement.

Persepolis' columns grew larger, they had to be over twenty metres tall, and I could see archways and the winged bullgods of the main gate, all raised above the surrounding plain on a high stone platform.

In a clump of flowering trees near the ruins was a small guest lodge. The owner gave me a jug of iced water; ah, there's nothing as good as cold water, then tea; and although he had no room for me he arranged for one of the management to move out of his room so that I could stay. Later, having said goodbye to the boy and his horse, I went out to look at the ruins.

The king who followed soon after Cyrus was Darius; he wanted his own personal capital so he built Persepolis, and the city was added to by Xerxes and Artaxerxes. But it was Darius who was the real genius; a benevolent and progressive imperialist. Once he had firmed up his empire in a military way he turned to its administration, taking Cyrus' improvised schemes and perfecting them.

At Persepolis Darius claimed the apron of a sacred limestone mountain and had a massive platform built extending from it, above the level of the plain. The platform merges into the shoulder of the mountain, joining man and nature.

Winged bulls over five metres tall flank the entrance, the pair facing outward across the plain have animals' heads, while those facing the city have human faces. This, the Gate of Xerxes, leads into an open area big enough for small armies to camp. Beyond, massive stone double staircases go up to palaces and the Apadana, or Audience Hall, with pillars almost twenty metres high; their tops had borne double capitals of sculpted animal heads.

The nearby Hall of 100 Pillars used to have a ceiling of cedar from Lebanon, with the Zoroastrian scriptures written in gold and silver on 12,000 tanned oxhides. The columns had originally been covered in painted plaster that glittered with jewels.

Darius' Palace had massive stone trilithon doorways, of monolithic slab lintels on two uprights, their interior surfaces carved with lifesize men fighting griffins, and lions giving allegiance. Eighteen trilithons are still standing, their themes of attendants and godly blessings. The palace is made of darker rock than the rest of Persepolis, its good state of preservation and high-polished finish due to it being formerly covered in mud. Achaemenian monumental art had reached its peak in Darius' reign; Xerxes continued by translating into stone his own megalomania.

But it is the staircases themselves that command attention. Sloping shallowly enough to allow horses up at a walk or canter, the massive eastern stairway of the Apadana has a carved stone frieze showing a procession of subjects from over twenty

nations, being ushered into court by Medes, recognisable by
their rounded hats. The subjects bring gifts and tribute as
diverse and exotic as the peoples: weapons, jewels, dishes,
textiles, specialities of their lands including livestock, two-
humped Bactrian camels being brought from near China and
dromedaries from Arabia; by the end of Darius' reign, twenty-
nine races were pledged to him in allegiance.

Then I paid attention to what I had really come to Persepolis
for, to see if there are any miniature Caspian horses in these
lines of people and their livestock. Many horses are shown, in
correct proportion to everything else on the frieze; some of the
breeds are as tall as men's shoulders, others smaller with long
manes; cobs with hogged manes and steppe horse noses, bulging foreheads, different conformation and characteristics; and
the men who brought the horses came from various tribes, as
illustrated by their clothes and helmets.

The sight planted the thought in my mind that I'd like to go
and look at the Kurdish Arabs in their native land. But Kurdistan
is remote and I doubted there would be time for a visit since I
also wanted to see the Assassins' Valley area.

Then I spotted a pair of miniature Caspians, pulling a chariot
with a cloaked charioteer, and on another staircase Caspians
are again shown, this time pulling a cart with a delegation of
bearded men carrying jars and urns. The Caspians are unmis-
takable; donkeys have donkeys' ears, and Caspians have tiny
curved ears.

On the final step of that staircase is an African tribe from
Ethiopia, men with frizzy hair bringing a large elephant's tusk
and leading a strange animal that looks like an outsize hyena;
it was probably a giraffe, long-necked with a sloping back.

The architecture of Persepolis is something that hits you face
on with its impact of strength, but there is nothing subtle about
it. Gone is the restraint of Pasargad, this was designed to make
mortals feel awed and humbled. The detail and technical skill
are repetitious and regimented, their purpose to highlight
power not beauty.

Leaving the palace I followed the contour of the hillside and
explored tombs cut in a black polished rock face veined with
white quartz. The cool interiors were a relief from the heat,
and one contained a massive stone sarcophagus carved with
attendant figures. I arrived back at the main ruins as the sun
set in a cloudless orange sky, and a mullah began his call to

prayer in a distant village. I listened as the sun's colours faded from the walls the Achaemenians had built 1,200 years before the arrival of Islam.

At the guest house people were chanting prayers in the corridor. My supper was rice and kebab; someone was singing outside, a traditional Persian ballad.

The next morning I went up to the ruins again. The only other tourists there were a few Iranian families, their raven-shaped women stood out starkly against the blinding glare of sun on pale stone. Some of the *chadoors* were lighter colours but always sober. While sitting in the shade of Darius' Palace I talked to one group from Tehran, and when we took some photographs they laughed because I pushed back my headscarf. Two of their women then pushed theirs back and shook out their hair. They said the *chadoor* makes their hair feel limp and smell bad. Afterwards I left my scarf pushed off my face but was ticked off by the curator for not being properly covered.

10   Trouble at the centre of the world

Shiraz has become a characterless modern city, and for me its main charm was the delightful family I happened to meet and stay with. They were a young married couple, a sister, a mother and five assorted aunts. Mozhgan, the sister, took me around the city and we visited the tomb of the famous poet Harvesan who died about a thousand years ago, but whose grave is still strewn with flower petals. Mozhgan and I drank iced grape juice in a cool bazaar teahouse with a fountain and singing birds. Shiraz used to produce two or three excellent wines, but the cellars have been closed by Khomeni's regime. The vines now only produce fruit, juice and raisins.

Supper at the family house was delicious (it was a relief to be off goat's curds), and we ate out in the yard, sitting on a thick Persian carpet. Especially good was the soup, *horosh bademjam*, made with pasta, vegetables and tomato; and one of the puddings, iced *baludeh*, which is pasta worms jellied in sweet syrup.

For coolness I slept out with a quilt in the yard, and by morning it was almost cold. Sleeping out around me were various aunts, a cat and her three kittens which played for most of the night in a pile of dry leaves. When I left in the morning, Mozhgan presented me with a necklace of woody seeds which smell good if you rub them between the palms of your hands.

I was now intending to go by bus to the Firuzabad area for it is the *qishlaq* (winter home) of Qashgai nomads, and has some interesting historical sites, but it turned into an abortive trip. Qashgai nomads are one of the most important, advanced and wealthiest tribes of Iran. Their origins are unclear but their language is Turkic. Reza Shah tried to break the power of the nomadic tribes by a scheme of enforced settlement, but nomadic hygiene depends on moving campsites from time to time, and the nomads' herds died, unable to exist without migration. It was only when meat became scarce in the cities that the Shah had to relax his policy, but not before most of their livestock had died. After the abdication of the last Shah, the Qashgai had forced the Iranian army out of their lands, and withdrew to rebuild their herds.

Plains followed gorges, the bus stopped for passengers to buy sugar-apples at an orchard. The road was slow, much was dirt road since the new road is not complete. My neighbour said the new road is unlikely to be finished for years because the workers have been called up to fight in the war.

A Sassanian city had been built at Firuzabad, circular to symbolise its position as the centre of the world. It is said that the three wise men had set out from somewhere around here bearing gifts for the birth of Jesus.

My first resolve was to hire a horse, knowing that the Qashgai are excellent horse-breeders, famed for their Darashuris; some stallions are said to have pedigrees dating back four hundred years. Many died during the ban on migration, but I was sure I'd find some sort of horse. However, the people in Firuzabad said there were no horses available. I couldn't get any sensible answers. Then a man walked up, short and balding but with an air of assurance and he seemed to speak some English. He took me to his family house for tea and water melon, then asked for my passport and began questioning me intensively about my journey.

He went away, so I taught his daughters to play noughts and crosses, until I heard the telephone ring and the man came back saying that he was going to drive me to the Revolutionary Guards. Why? To show them my passport. The man was all smiles but they were slimy ones.

I had no choice but to do as told, and in the police station I kept my un-socked feet tucked out of sight. I had to sit like that so long I got pins-and-needles, but didn't want to stretch my legs in a roomful of Revolutionary Guards. The slimy bald man was also there, smiling importantly and telling them everything I had said about my trip, but he wouldn't tell me what the problem was. I kept pointing out that I was only a tourist and my passport was in perfect order, and he kept smiling and nodding.

At 1 p.m. the guards confiscated my passport, and the bald man took me back to his house to have lunch and await further developments. I noticed several pictures of Khomeni on the walls, and when I asked what he thought of Khomeni, he said

Khomeni was very good. Out of the many people of different backgrounds in Iran that I had asked this same question, he was the only one who liked Khomeni, and what a creep.

At 3 p.m. the Revolutionary Guards telephoned to say bring her back, so back we went. I was locked up and left to stew. Then the boss of the guards and a mean scar-faced man came in to say I could not stay in Firuzabad, I must go back to Shiraz immediately and report to the police station there.

Playing the indignant and inane tourist I replied that I didn't mind leaving on the evening bus to Shiraz but now I was going to see the local historical monuments. He tried to refuse permission but gave way under my barrage of inanity. I was released and my passport returned but the bald man took me to the bus stop and said I must catch the next bus out.

Fortunately a taxi came past so I quickly arranged to hire it for a tour of the ruins on the plain, which would fill the rest of the afternoon. This is the site of Gur, the city Ardeshir built 2,000 years ago on the battleground of his greatest victory; his palace is still partially standing.

Our first stop was four kilometres out on dirt tracks at Mumareh to look at a massive solid stone tower with no entrance or interior. Visible from afar, its top would have been a great lookout point if there had been a staircase. I wondered what it had been built for. Scrambling around I disturbed a small brown fox which fled, and watched a young eagle making a test flight from its nest in the tower. The taxi driver saw it too, and climbed up to the nest where he found the eagle's brother who hadn't yet learned to fly. The youngster leapt from his grasp and plummeted to the ground. I hoped it would fly away, but it immobilised itself by standing on one of its own wings. The driver recaptured it and put it in the taxi. He said he would train it as a hunting bird.

We drove through a Qashgai village but when I got out of the taxi to talk to some women an old crone screamed abuse at me; not a friendly place. So we drove on another five kilometres to the main site I wanted to see, the ruins of the Palace of Ardeshir. Built circa AD 300 and reputed to have not only the Islamic world's oldest surviving dome of any real size, it also contains the first example of a squinch; a structural feature which makes a square able to support a dome, thus it is a landmark in the development of architectural technique.

Entering the palace I found myself in a dark row of three big

Above: A fourth-century Cappadocian rock church, now exposed by rockfall.
Below: An Ürgüp bazaar seller identifies his wares. 'My name is Erik.'
Below right: The *chadoor* as an aid to flirtation.

Above: Turkoman carpet-weaving at Ghara Tepeh Sheikh.
Above right: The matriarch whose *alachekh* Louise Firouz was buying.
Below: Inside, her sons played bamboo flutes.

Above: Baluchi girls baking bread in a clay oven. *Above right:* Kooros shows me the entrance to his *qanat.* The windlass is to raise the buckets of sand during dredging.
Below: The old summer home of Kooros' grandfather.

The road to Quetta.
The juggler whose monkeys kept teasing the porcupine.

I ride past the Roman Emperor Valerian grovelling to Shapur I of Persia at Naksh-i-Rustam. Part of the frieze on the grand stairway, Persepolis. A pair of miniature Caspians are pulling the cart bottom **right**.

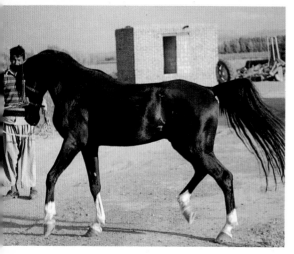

Issa's black Plateau Persian stallion.

A superb Kurdish Arab.

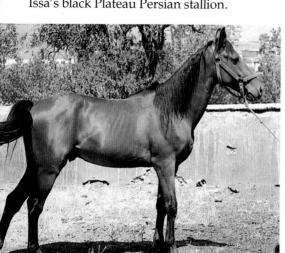

A typically long backed Turkoman racehorse.

The author riding a Turkoman racehorse.

Ardeshir's pride and joy, wearing a fly-band.

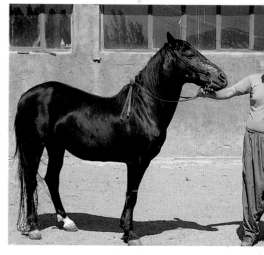

A short legged Baseri Arab in Kurdistan.

On horseback you can pick any direction through the mountains.
Saying farewell to my hostess at Gümüslü.

Lake Van, and Aqhtamar island with its tenth-century church.
A lush camp-site.

Above: This church at Beş Kilise, near Digor, was used as a sundial.
Below: Keyif being shod with the traditional closed shoes and studs.
Below right: The ruined church at Çamleyamak.

My memory of Keyif, with Mount Ararat on the horizon.

Above: Delicious Iranian home cooking with Esak's family in Isfahan.
Below: An Assassins' castle strategically placed for plundering the trade routes of the Elburz Mountains.
Below right: Cifte Minareli Medrese with its rival towers.

Çirit riders at Erzurum fair.

One of the village dance teams.

An old couple from Gümüslü.

Left: I thought the pelican was stuffed until it pecked me.
Below: Eid celebrations: a contest of markmanship at Khan Mahterzai.
Bottom: The wrestling match.

Aziz's family making butter in a goatskin churn.

Turkoman women put up their *alachekh* at Ghara Tepeh Sheikh.
Louise and Narcy Firouz demonstrate the difference in size between miniature
Caspians and other horses.

A Baluchi nomad village of palmleaf tents, some plastered with mud.
The ancient capital of Bam, with the modern city beyond.

halls each domed with a hole open to the sky at the top of each dome. The central dome is the highest. The eastern one is partly fallen and in sunlight I could see how the squinches fuse the shape and surface from square to round. Turning to the west dome I climbed up fallen debris on to the first storey, and up further rubble to the second storey then on to the central dome's baked mud brick and mortar, where I lay looking down into the hall from above: deep, dark and giddy-making. But the dome still felt strong.

Looking over the courtyard gave me a commanding view of its layout; barrel-vaulted rooms and chambers with archways; their rough stonework and mortar construction was once covered in mud plaster with ornamental mouldings around the archways. To the east I could see a perfectly circular spring of fresh water, a deep azure pool encompassed by a ring of reeds, with a stream flowing from it. A group of Qashgai women arrived to bathe. They bathed fully dressed and kept their heads covered, lying flat out in the stream. Then they shook out the hems of their multi-layered skirts, and flicked their wet hair forward into ear-set pigtails, and went back to work in their village.

The young eagle had escaped out of the taxi's window. I wasn't sorry, and the driver returned to Firuzabad just in time for me to catch the last bus to Shiraz. Later that evening at my friends' house we examined my passport and visa for flaws.

'I entered Iran on the 17th.'.

'It's now the 31st,' Mozhgan added.

'No,' I countered, 'it's only the 21st.' And we argued about the date until an aunt pointed out that the Iranian calendar is different from the western one used in my passport. The current Iranian year was 1365, to our 1986.

As instructed, I went to the police headquarters at 9 a.m. next morning to be told my passport and visa were fine and that the *pastares* (Revolutionary Guards) were a load of illiterate oafs. I was tempted to agree.

In search of a beautiful city I went by bus to Isfahan, which is said to rate alongside Rome and Paris as one of the world's most splendid. I arrived at 5 a.m., crossing the river and seeing the amber glow of streetlights mixing with the red dawn.

What can one do in a city at 5 a.m? I walked back to the river called Zende Rud which means River of Life, and contemplated its three oldest bridges. At Khaju Bridge the water is split into many channels like an ancient multi-gated weir. People and bicycles were crossing on their way to work, and down below a boy was running along the underwater ledges feeling for fish with his hands. I sat nearby and ate a breakfast of boiled eggs, bread and apples.

Upriver the next bridge is Pol-i-Chubi, with pointed stone arches, and further up is Si-o-Seh Pol which means thirty-three arches but I counted more than that. Apart from its series of arches over the river channels there are two many-arched pedestrian walks flanked by rows of blind arches. While sitting counting them, I met a young man called Esak, a factory worker who could speak good English. He told me it was his day off and so he could take me wherever I wished to go.

'I want to shake the Trembling Minarets,' I answered, having heard that if you shake one of these twin minarets the other will also begin to tremble. We found the fourteenth-century minarets in a park in the city's suburbs, but unfortunately they were closed for repair. So we hitched a lift three kilometres further to the city's outskirts where I had read of an ancient fire temple. Because this had not been commercialised as a tourist attraction, we had to crawl through a wire mesh fence before beginning a long steep climb up the tall plug of rock.

On the summit's edge are clustered the ruins of several buildings and on the highest point is the great fireplace, an eight-arched cylindrical edifice four metres across. It was a superb lookout point. Esak and I sat in the shade of the fire temple and talked for two hours, discussing all the questions that people are sometimes afraid to answer in case they are overheard. This province, Fars, being in the war zone means that Esak's thoughts often dwell on the war; the net of conscription is being tightened and the period has been extended to two years. One would be lucky to live that long, since conscripts are used to create a human wave running at the Iraqi enemy to cause confusion and be shot down, making way for the Iranian regular troops. Iraq is also using the ugliest of chemical warfare.

Families who lose a son are allowed to shop in Martyr Stores, where goods are sold that are not available to the general public. Martyrdom is extolled by Khomeni, as in the pictures I had already seen lining the streets of many towns. Recruits used to be issued with a 'key to heaven' to hang around their neck. Some of the 'volunteers' are only 14-year-old boys, who are enrolled by their mullahs – one way of getting rid of the trouble-makers.

Esak's brother had been sent to fight but after a month he had fled with four friends, managing to cross the border into Turkey. Reaching Istanbul they had obtained forged passports and were now in East Germany, seeking refugee status in the West. As to the actual progress of the war, it was looking bad for Iran because their five major oil ports had been bombed, yet their spring offensive had been a success.

As for the young men who weren't on call-up, they weren't having a ball. The ban on music, dancing, and alcohol, being forbidden to walk with young women in public, or even drink tea with women, makes social life very drab. But Esak told me he was lucky to have a job as unemployment was running high.

We went to his family house for lunch, twelve of us sitting around a floor cloth spread with dishes of chicken in rich tomato sauce, *mast,* green salad, and bread. Everyone was talking and laughing, I said I would certainly remember them for their noise and laughter level, and Esak explained that they were happy to entertain a tourist since they hadn't met one for ten years. Their father was a simple man with a kindly face and ready smile, he had struggled to save his money so that Esak could learn English.

After lunch we broke some of Khomeni's taboos by turning on a cassette player and dancing. The music was Persian and the girls wanted to give me a dancing lesson. Their love of dance was so great that the daughter clearing up lunch was found dancing with the dish cloth and soapsuds. One daughter didn't dance because she was eight months pregnant, and miserable since her husband had been taken prisoner by the Iraqis and she was unlikely ever to see him again.

Late afternoon Esak and I went to the Friday Mosque. He didn't know why I wanted to see it, he had to pray there every week and said it wasn't interesting; but when I set out he insisted on coming too. Properly covered women may visit mosques, but are generally forbidden to pray except in a curtained or hidden area reserved for them.

The late sun made the mosque's tilework glow and threw shadows from every angle of the entrance portals. An eleventh-century building, there are entrances on three sides of the square and the interior is hollow sounding and empty but for pigeons roosting; its ceiling is a geometrical puzzle of small domes, crescents and curved triangles filling angles and creating bigger domes. The squinch had come to town; and become far more sophisticated than those at Ardeshir's Palace. I'd never imagined so many squinches all in one building.

There was still plenty of time before sunset, and my bus wouldn't leave until 10 p.m., so I dragged Esak to the Maidan-i-Imam, the Royal Square, an open space twice as large as Moscow's Red Square, flanked by mosques, palaces and a royal grandstand (Ali Qapu) for watching wrestlers, gladiators, and polo being played in the arena; polo is reputed to have originated in Persia, a refinement of games the nomadic tribes had played using decapitated goats. When a youthful Alexander the Great succeeded his father, the Emperor of Persia sent him a polo mallet, as a message that he should stick to such sports and leave warmongering alone.

The Maidan and its surrounding mosques were built by Shah Abbas in the seventeenth century and, in contrast to the intricate mosaics of Isfahan's older monuments, the walls are covered with large colourfully painted and enamelled tiles. Some tiles are glazed and some are mat so that as one moves, their highlights change.

Twilight was fading by the time we reached Abbas' harem, set in a park which was locked but the caretaker let us in to see the Palace of Forty Pillars, so named because its twenty pillars are reflected in an ornamental pond. There are murals of Abbas picnicking with some playmates (his harem was reported to have housed several hundred women and over two hundred boys) and drinking wine, one of his milder vices.

Although I am not a city person and had only gone to Isfahan since it was en route and I felt I ought to stop there, albeit briefly, yet it impressed me as deserving its reputation and I carry with me the memory of its friendship and fading opulence.

11 Into the war zone

One hundred and fifty kilometres west of Tehran, where the Elburz Mountains rise back towards the Caspian Sea, are the Valleys of the Assassins. It is in this region that Narcy and Louise Firouz have their second ranch, and I had a standing invitation to visit them when my travels took me back west again.

The Assassins flourished for 200 years from the late eleventh century and were notorious as hired killers. The sect started out led by Hasan Sabbah (a school fellow of Omar Khayyam) against the Seljuks who were trying to force people to accept Sunni Islam. In a ruthless holy war, the hard-core extremist Shi'ites retreated into mountain strongholds. The Sabbah sect built over 350 castles, and chose the one on Alamut Rock to be their headquarters, for taking revenge on Seljuk targets. The name Assassins come from *hashishin* (eater of hashish) which their leaders supplied to indoctrinate the recruits. The Assassins were feared for their coldblooded ability to stalk and kill, spreading terror, while they themselves welcomed death as an entrance to heavenly paradise. It sounds rather like the Khomeni martyrs and their keys to heaven.

Remembering the barn at Ghara Tepeh Sheikh, I didn't expect to find a ranch house and was amused to see that one was hurriedly being built. It even had electricity, although it wasn't working, due to a power cut. Iraqi bombers had recently hit some of Iran's power plants. It was lovely to be with Louise and Narcy again and to have the opportunity of riding fine horses over the foothills of the Elburz Mountains.

My mare was Shanaza, a superb black Yamoud Turkoman, and she was a pacer, which means she knew how to move front and back legs on each side together, instead of diagonally. It was fun to put her through her paces, collected and extended. She could also trot, which some pacers cannot. With ears pricked and nostrils flared, Shanaza enjoyed looking at her surroundings. I felt she was sharing my pleasure. I let her speed into a gallop and it felt marvellous to race along the cliff tops in the wind. All along a canyon's rim was cultivated with wheat, white-gold laced with purple flowering vetch, and I noticed how the wind through unripe wheat makes a different sound to that when the crop is ripe. Here in the hills the season was less advanced than it had been at Ghara Tepeh Sheikh. But the mulberries were ripe. Ducking under low branches, they rained down on me and Shanaza. These are white mulberries which here are dried for winter and eaten like sweets.

As we progressed up a dry sandy streambed and over more hills I became aware of a scattered line of villages hidden in valleys, fertile patches in the dry brown land, and yet more villages tucked into folds beneath the mountains. All this area was the Assassins' stomping-ground; it was a shame there were no castles, but according to Narcy, even the famous castle on Alamut Rock has crumbled to a few fragments of wall.

Nowadays the region is a haunt of Majuhedin insurgents who have been known to kill local Revolutionary Guards when given a chance. The spirit of the Assassins carries on. Another visitor to this area had been Dame Freya Stark. Louise had met her a couple of times, and so had I in England. One piece of her philosophy that impressed me was when she said, 'The great and almost only comfort about being a woman is that one can always pretend to be more stupid than one is and no one will be surprised.' This is a technique which has helped me out of a number of tight corners in different parts of the world from China to Africa, but it seemed not always to be working in Iran where the Revolutionary Guards tended to be even more stupid themselves! Freya Stark had also ridden by mule along part of the Euphrates and on another occasion to the headwaters of the Tigris in south-east Turkey. I hoped to cross her tracks again later.

I had only been with Louise and Narcy four days when late one afternoon a Kurdish friend of Louise called at the stables and mentioned that he would be driving up to Kurdistan the following day. He offered to take me there and show me the best of Kurdistan's horses. What a wonderful opportunity. I had to be ready to leave within the hour.

I was sad to leave Louise and Narcy but, as they said, Ardeshir's offer was too good to be missed. We drove in his pick-up truck to Qazvin, a town below the foot of the Assassins'

Valley. With his few words of English and my few words of Farsi we managed to communicate quite well, though I wondered if I had totally misunderstood when he took me to a hotel and wouldn't let me pay for my room. He left me to wash and said he would be back later. But I felt sure he had no ulterior motives, Kurds are known to be men of honour.

He did come back, to take me out to supper. Then he shook my hand and said he would collect me at 5 a.m. to start our journey to Kurdistan.

At 6 a.m. Ardeshir arrived by car and we set off, crossing the level cultivated plains along the foot of the western Elburz, flat to Zanjan then north-west into hills and open rolling country-side. We stopped at a roadside café for breakfast of eggs and thin sheets of bread, and tea. Some donkeys trotted past, so laden with hay I could see only their hooves and noses. One boy was standing on his donkey's rump, there was nowhere to sit. As it went along the donkey snatched mouthfuls to eat from its load.

Continuing up mountains we crossed an undulating highland plateau that had clashing colours of mustard yellow thorny flowers, pink lupins, purple flowering lucerne, and rocks of pale green, burnt sienna-mauve and honey-gold. Occasional hamlets of mud cottages broke the emptiness, and dung, dried for fuel in long pats, was stacked in tall conical mounds.

Our route passed through northern Luristan, where peasant-farmers regularly turn up treasure troves and bronzes of supreme quality from old tombs whose whereabouts are a jealously guarded secret.

We entered Kurdistan; although we hadn't made any steep ascents the land had rolled endlessly upward, I could tell the altitude changes by the hiss of air whenever I opened my water flask.

Villages were now made from red mud, some of brick, their flat roofs loaded with drying hay. There were old crumbling forts and new Revolutionary Guard forts. The fighting which goes on here is not only the Iranians against the Iraqis, it's also the Revolutionary Guard, the *pastares*, against the Kurds. The *pastares* make the law from 9 a.m. to 6 p.m., then the law of the Kurds takes over. Ardeshir assured me that, in his company, I would be safe from both types.

From Kurds I had met in the past, and in London, I'd learned that their trouble is in being a nation without a country, and as a race of twenty million they claim to be the third most numerous people of the Middle East. Their people are divided between Iran, Iraq, Syria, Turkey, and a few remain in Russia.

The Kurds got a raw deal in the past when Britain, America, and Russia all promised to help them in their fervent wish to form an independent state. This was to be in return for fighting favours; the Kurds fulfilled their part but the other powers reneged on the deal. The treaty of Sèvres in 1920 agreed to grant Kurdish autonomy, but it was overthrown by Atatürk who didn't want to let go of any land.

At a T-junction we turned south beside a stream, the land became more mountainous as the stream wove between crags, yet pastoral with men scything hay, and unsettling with soldiers in tin hats carrying machine guns. They were guarding the roads, their vehicles had armoured guns mounted on the back, but the men seemed friendly enough. Some of the Kurds were also carrying rifles slung on their backs.

Winding upward, we drove past cerulean lakes and enjoyed long vistas over valleys and other lakes, patches of farmland in the vastness of open grazing, outcrops of rock and tall clumps of cobalt blue forget-me-nots. Up and up to Sanandaj where we stopped for lunch of *arpusht*, a kind of soup with meat, tomato, potato and chick-peas, eaten by shredding masses of bread into it. Sanandaj is a purely Kurdish town and men stroll around in baggy trousers caught at the waist with a sash; on their heads they wear a skull cap or a tall cap with a turban wrapped around it. Most turbans are silver and black with a long fringe. Women seldom wear the *chadoor*, preferring their traditional baggy trousers, shirts, and headscarves threaded with glitter.

'Let's go and see some horses,' Ardeshir suggested, and we drove up to a farm where the owner was away but an old man showed us around: thirty sheep, fifty long-legged bantam chickens, and two superb Kurdish stallions, standing at 14.2 h.h. and of slightly rakish build. At another farm we were shown two much stockier Kurdish stallions, 14 h.h. and barrel chested, with heavy heads yet distinctly Arabian flared nostrils and bulging foreheads. The owner valued them each at 100,000 tumen (£1000). I photographed one stallion, the other was too vicious to be taken outside; he stood tied by his head and one back foot. To ride these horses the owner uses a traditional Kurdish bit with a spike and ring; the ring goes in the mouth and around the back of the chin, to hold the tongue down and give extra power to the spike. The spike is flattened, not pointed, and I doubt it's cruel since no gentler bit would have a chance of stopping such a horse, and if a man values his horses he would not wish to damage them. The tack room smelt of well-kept leather, treated with beeswax since no saddle-soap was available. The saddles were conventional though decorated with tassels and pompoms, and the stirrups had a long tread with triangular sides.

We sat talking and eating water-melon out in his courtyard by a pond. The fountain made a soothing noise. When I asked why the house was only half-built, the owner shrugged and replied, 'Khomeni.' Wealthy people are wise to keep a low profile and have nothing that looks worth confiscating. Farmers who do well are likely to be penalised, so this one had turned simply self-sufficient using one acre to grow his grapevines, strawberries, apples, peaches, apricots, cherries, pumpkins, potatoes, tomatoes and roses.

He said that there are not many Kurdish Arabs around now because most have been shot and killed by the *pastares*, to stop them being used for terrorist activity. *Pastares* don't usually know how to ride, and they're at a disadvantage fighting Kurds on horseback.

From there we went to a stables near the Hamadan road where I borrowed a Kurdish stallion for a ride. At first the owner tried to dissuade me because of recent local shootings, but I said I wouldn't go far. The stables were set in hilly wheatland. I rode over the hills and now that the wheat was partly harvested there was freedom to canter across the stubble. Around the back of some hills I met five horsemen, local Kurds carrying baggage and babies on three Kurdish horses and two large mules. Their saddles were all of the donkey type, big and cumbersome on a padded wooden frame which gives a rider no grip on the horse. It must make for good balance.

Later by a river I met some boys herding cattle across to the opposite bank, so I rounded up the strays for them before heading west, galloping on open ground between rounded hills. The craggy outcrops on their summits looked like natural fortresses, and when I rode up on to the hilltops I could see that several had army lookout camps in current use. Reining in, I ducked out of sight behind the hills. I was enjoying the ride, the horse had a marvellous untiring canter; at some huts

I noticed about ten women sitting on a roof watching me; Kurdish women can ride, but these looked too fat, their shiny scarves and dresses catching the evening light. It was already past 7 o'clock, and the warnings about lawlessness rang in my mind but it wouldn't be dark until 8.30. When I heard rifle shots followed by a second burst of fire, I turned for home.

Back at the stables the men brought out their finest horse, and everyone stood well clear as he lunged out, a magnificent palomino stallion, 15 h.h. and strongly built. He was saddled but whenever a man tried to get on his back he reared up high, striking forward with his front hooves. However, Kurds tend to be good with horses and one man managed to stay on long enough to treat us to a spectacular display of rearing, made all the more wild by the craggy backdrop of hills lit by the setting sun.

Ardeshir and I left, the roads were rough and twilight was nearly gone. The way led through a river, we drove through the water but while climbing the far bank the car's motor spluttered and died. 'No problem,' said Ardeshir opening the hood, and in an impressively short time he got the engine going again. Back on the proper road we had an accident; Ardeshir was tired and the windscreen so dirty that he failed to see the kerb and trees until too late. He slammed on the brakes and we skidded over the kerb into some small trees. No major damage and fortunately we were only shaken not hurt.

Ardeshir decided it was too dangerous for us to stay in Sanandaj. There was due to be fighting that night, so he insisted we drive 200 kilometres to his family's village. The plan seemed thwarted when we found an army barricade across the road, but we got through, and at another road block there were *pastares* who Ardeshir said were very bad, but he talked our way through that as well. On the winding mountain route Ardeshir turned off the car's headlights and said it was safer to drive without lights. I said it was definitely not. He was already very tired and the moon had not yet risen.

To keep him awake we sang songs, taking turns with English ballads and Kurdish ones. His had long droning wordless parts becoming tuneful in their choruses. But we obviously weren't going to manage 200 kilometres, and finally about halfway we pulled in beside a river and went to sleep. A cold night, luckily we each had a blanket. Sharing one would have been a problem, since in his sleep Ardeshir kicked and snorted, and gnashed his teeth. It was rather like sharing a stall with a Kurdish stallion.

I didn't get much sleep and was awake at first light. We found an early-opening café for breakfast of *mast*, bread and sweet tea; the other people there were engrossed in talk of an incident during the night about ten kilometres from where we had slept. But Ardeshir said it wasn't anything important.

We continued our drive, the scenery was the typical Kurdistan hilly highlands with streams bordered by cultivation, pasturelands above, and a soldier on sentry duty on each crag. During the next hundred kilometres we saw many of them and passed through several road blocks. As we went along I realised that Ardeshir has a very gentle nature, in the way he swerved to avoid hitting a frog, and was distressed by killing a mouse which ran under our wheels.

By lunchtime we had arrived in Mahabad, where we found a café in the bazaar with *arpusht* soup, and Ardeshir met some friends. Two of them, rather dashing young Kurds, offered to show us some good horses eleven kilometres away and although I told Ardeshir I had taken enough photographs of horses, he was keen to go anyway.

At a road block in the mountains just outside Mahabad we were all detained by *pastares* and arrested. The two dashing young Kurds were blindfolded and taken away. An armed guard pushed Ardeshir and me into the car and made him drive to the Revolutionary Guard HQ in Mahabad.

When next I saw the other two they were sitting still blindfolded in a guarded tent at the headquarters, a yard with high walls and coils of barbed wire. My baggage was opened in the yard and everything was strewn in the dirt. The guards searched minutely through it all and, when I tried to help by explaining things, they sent me to sit in the guarded tent. Ardeshir was taken for interrogation, then the two men were led away, and I was left to stew for several hours.

I closed my eyes but was sharply reprimanded, sleep was not permitted. At one point my guard was a boy of about thirteen years old, fingering his machine gun restlessly and refusing my requests for him to fetch his seniors or someone who could speak English. The only successful request was for the loo. On the way back I saw a flashy jeep enter the yard and persisted in my argument to see the boss; this attracted their attention and I reached an officer. The next five hours followed an almost familiar pattern, similar to my first arrest in Gonbad but with the addition of continual searches.

However in the searches they ignored my diaries, and were mainly interested in the pictures on my old tourist map of Quetta and my photographs of home. At times I felt angry and so helpless but kept my temper, even when I was blindfolded and locked up. All my luggage and papers were confiscated, Ardeshir's car was confiscated, and I had no idea what was happening to my companions.

It was a twenty-one-hour ordeal. The root of the problem seemed to be that this was a war zone and the *pastares* didn't have any specific work to do but terrorise the Kurds. It didn't ease the situation when Iran took an overnight beating in the fighting thirty kilometres away on the Iraqi border. Reinforcements poured through Mahabad the next morning, and during the chaos my release papers were signed.

Then came the hard part. I had to explain that I couldn't leave until my three Kurdish friends and the car were also released. Not a popular idea; from the *pastares'* expressions it looked likely I would be re-arrested. But perseverance and dignity were the keys, and by 2 p.m. Ardeshir and I were in the car speeding out of town.

Ardeshir had refused to let me catch a bus to Tabriz, he said he wanted to visit his cousin who lived there. At the village where we stopped for lunch he suggested with a smile, 'Let's go and see some horses.' So we did.

Then we drove past the largest salt lake in Iran, Lake Urmia, took a wrong turn and got stuck in a deep putrid green puddle. The car sucked water up its exhaust and choked to a halt in the deepest part of the puddle. Ardeshir managed to open the hood and dry the spark plugs without getting his feet wet, he is a remarkable man.

When the time came to take leave of him in Tabriz, we looked at each other and burst out laughing. We had shared a slice of life together, and had developed the bond of those who share adversity. We shook hands and said farewell.

When Ardeshir had gone I felt forlorn and couldn't muster much enthusiasm for sightseeing in Tabriz. The city seemed to be in a state of military alert and I had problems finding a hotel which would accept me. The *otogar*, where I went to buy a ticket for the morrow's bus to the Turkish border, was very crowded but some soldiers helped me to obtain the last available seat.

During the bus trip I rebuked myself for feeling gloomy about leaving Iran. Had I forgotten that I only came to Iran because eastern Turkey had been too wintry for horse-riding? Now it was early July, summer should have reached there and I was about to begin fulfilling the original purpose of my journey.

Crossing the border back into Turkey, the atmosphere in immigration was as if clouds cleared and sun shone through. 'You may take off your *mantau* and your scarf. Your permit is valid for three months. Welcome to Turkey.'

Five

TRAVELS WITH KEYIF

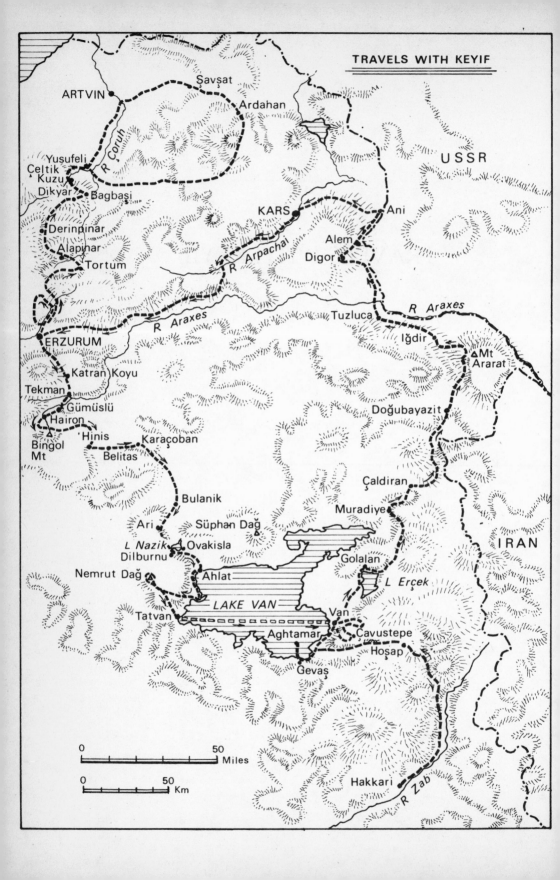

TRAVELS WITH KEYIF

ARTVIN Şavşat
Ardahan

USSR

Yusufeli
Çeltik
Kuzu
Dikyar Bağbaşı
Derinpınar
Alapınar
Tortum

R Çoruh

KARS
Ani
Alem
Digor

R Arpaçaı

R Araxes

Tuzluca
Iğdir

R Araxes

ERZURUM

Mt
Ararat

Katran Koyu
Tekman
Gümüşlü
Hairon
Hinis
Bingöl
Mt

Karaçoban
Belitas

Doğubayazit

Bulanik

Çaldiran

Ari
Süphan Dağ
L Nazik Ovakisla
Dilburnu
Nemrut Dağ Ahlat

Muradiye

IRAN

Golalan
L Erçek

LAKE VAN

Tatvan

Van

Aghtamar Çavuştepe
Hosap
Gevaş

0   50
                  Miles

0   50
                  Km

Hakkari

R Zab

12 Horse-trading days

Arriving back in Erzurum I went straight to Sema's apartment, where I received a warm welcome; how I appreciated Sema and her family, it was so much nicer to stay with them than in an impersonal hotel. What I liked about Sema was her fresh open mind and common sense. In the apartment lift I met covered women showing only their eyes, and modern women who are materialistic and fashion-conscious; Sema is neither. She loves nature and is close to the land. Her work in the agricultural department takes her to villages to try and organise crop management and stock-breeding programmes. She doesn't think that Turkish women work harder than men or that they are suppressed and exploited. She doesn't see it that way. And she entered enthusiastically into my plans to buy a horse.

She discovered that her office clerk's brother played çirit (pronounced jirit), a local horseback sport, and when his work finished for the day he took me to a nearby village where two çirit horses were for sale. Çirit, he told me, is a game where daredevil riders throw wooden javelins at each other and it has been traditional in this region since the Middle Asian steppe peoples settled here at the beginning of Turkish history. Çirit horses have short necks and strong bodies and are bred for their speed and ability to stop suddenly. I tried out both horses, they were equally fun to ride, though their mouths were hard as iron and when I looked I could see the sores and wounds from rough handling on the field of play. Though they were excitable to ride, the owner crouched under their bellies to show how docile they were, and I tested them by picking up their back hooves to see if they were difficult. But I couldn't afford the çirit horses, and one of them had a famous reputation. All I needed was a good travelling horse. Anyway, a valuable horse was more likely to be stolen.

Sema said she would find out which day the weekly bazaar took place. Meanwhile I explored the ancient corners of Erzurum. Some students, eager to practise their English, showed me the

Seljuk university dating from the thirteenth century where
students used to study astronomy, physics, maths and the Koran. They said you can identify any Seljuk building by the carved
eagle, and pointed to an eagle relief by the main gate.

The ancient dormitory which had housed the Seljuk students,
Çift Minareli Medrese, was built in 1253, a beautiful building
with elaborately incised scrollwork in stone. Its twin minarets
were fluted brick with square turquoise tiles, and the boys told
me their story: one minaret was built by a master craftsman and
the other by his apprentice. The one built by the youngster
looked better than that of his master, who became so upset he
climbed to the top of his minaret and threw himself to his death.

The dormitories were set in two storeys around a garden
courtyard. Pigeons and swallows swooped through arches decorated by chiselled arabesques. The raucous noise of a bugle-
trumpet went past outside in a truck. It was a marriage
procession taking a bride from her house to the groom's family.

At a shop for horse tack I looked at saddles, there were the
Spanish style used in Europe and the Ottoman style which was
a thick pad of stuffed leather. I'd tried one on a *çirit* horse and
didn't like the way it raised me above the horse's back. The
bridles in the shop had various fierce types of bit, versions of
the curb.

In the weekly bazaar there were three horses. One of them
had potential as a travelling horse but the men who gathered
around me were disparaging, and someone offered to bring
two of his own horses to add to my choice. These horses duly
arrived, galloping through the streets, and I tried them both.
One was uncomfortable, the other was a beauty. But his price
was far higher than I had thought of paying and I decided not
to rush into buying anything immediately.

I managed to find out the location and day of a trade fair
which only interests the Turks. Maybe I'd find a horse there,
but I had also heard there would be village dance groups, and
a game of *çirit*, which I was now longing to see.

On the afternoon of the fair I set off on foot. Sema was out
at work and it wasn't the sort of thing that would have appealed
to her mother or grandmother, so I went alone. The noise of a
procession filled the streets. It was twelve *çirit* players, and
when I asked one rider what time the game was due to begin
he dismounted and offered me his horse, so I rode to the fair
in the *çirit* procession.

At the gates I dismounted to join the throng on foot watching a local dance group, men and women, with musicians playing drums and the *zouna*, a sort of trumpet that sounds like a snake-charmer's pipe. Bitlis village dance team took over, wearing dark purple with gold sashes, men forming a human wall that surged and retreated, swinging and swaying with the music then parting and making pairs to battle with each other, slapping each other's hands with a force that must have stung.

Trabzon's male dance team looked incongruously like hell's angels with black clothes and boots, silver chains, and daggers. They danced a high stepping jig, their drummer whirled and in addition to drumsticks he used his elbows and knees, keeping the rhythm going all the while. Most drummers used one spoon-shaped stick which hit with a great thump, and a whippy twig which made a zinging noise. Van team's men wore red fezzes with yellow scarves around them, and embroidered waistcoats – their women had long flounced skirts and multi-coloured headdresses, only outshone by the Erzurum women in long velvet dresses with gold embroidery. They did a scarf-waving dance which was rather stately and genteel.

But in my opinion the Adiaman team were the best, in fezzes, baggy trousers and tops, women in woven dresses over baggy striped pantaloons, and white headgear Arab-style. One by one the girls were compelled by the drum rhythm to dance a solo whirling and wiggling in front of the drummer yet managing to escape before being trapped. The prettiest girl didn't escape, she danced to the drummer and ended bowing low in acceptance, a willing catch. For their harvesting dance the girls brought gourds of water to the men as they reaped the wheat with short scythes, dancing in pairs with agility and grace. I saw men playing the *saz*, too, a traditional eight-string guitar with deep bowl and metre-long neck. The only thing I didn't see was any other tourists – although the crowds were enormous, they were all Turks.

For me the high point of the festival was the display of *çirit*. Twenty-four horses charged into the arena, separating into two teams at different ends. One horseman galloped towards the centre and two from the other end came at full tilt towards him, waving poles of wood a metre long and looking as if they were going to throw them at the solo horseman. Which of course they were, and at about five metres distance one man threw his stick, javelin style, it hissed past missing the other rider, but his companion closed in fast and took aim. As he loosed the stick, travelling devastatingly fast, the target rider ducked and slid out of sight on the lee side of his horse. The crowd roared approval as the stick shot harmlessly above him.

Their roars were louder a moment later when a fourth horseman joined the fray and managed to hit a rider. The pole caught him in the back, he seemed unhurt but the hit gave three points to the other team. He was not 'out', you cannot be disqualified unless you hit the referee. Sticks that miss score three points for the other team. Every man is a target, especially after he's thrown his javelin and is defenceless. To escape he gallops back towards his team's end of the arena, taunting his opponents by waving his arms. Sometimes riders find themselves totally outnumbered by the opposing team, skill and speed are their only hope of escape. When a close-range hit is unavoidable, the men don't actually throw, but they gain points for 'could have hit'. Reaching their home end they can collect another stick. They raced up and down the arena, dust rose, and whenever there was a lull in play, drums and trumpets sounded to encourage the riders on.

In one team I recognised the horse I had ridden in the procession, and in the other was Sema's clerk's brother riding the famous horse I had tried out in the village.

A couple of times I saw the target rider manage to catch the stick being shot at him. The crowd loved it, though the rider doesn't gain points for the catch. Lost sticks are gathered by the three referees who dodge around the pitch. The game is as dangerous for them as for the horses, riders and the crowd, though a modern outdoor stadium has been built with protective wire mesh. An ambulance was waiting on standby.

On my way to Sema's office one day I met the owner of the fine grey stallion I'd tried out at the bazaar. As the horse paced down the street he looked superb; young and spirited, tassels swinging from his bridle and saddle. The man and I went to a teahouse to discuss my possible purchase of the horse: I was being reluctant but the man was insistent that if I bought his horse, I would never regret it. There was something persuasive about that. And I knew that he was an honest man, a well-respected figure as chairman of the *çirit* club. By this time I'd managed to bargain twenty per cent off his price, now making it 300,000 Turkish lire (£300), which would include the horse's tack. The bridle had beautifully beaded straps, its browband had a small round mirror inset in beadwork and four beaded tassels.

This horse wasn't in the same class as the best of Iranian Arabs, but by Turkish standards he was good-looking. His name was Keyif, meaning high-spirited. As to where Keyif and I should travel, I flipped a coin. This decided the journey should go first to Lake Van, about 200 kilometres to the south-east; we could then loop around the lake, and head north via Ararat and up into the north-east. It would take at least two months to ride that far.

13 Welcome to the feast

Dawn was hot and dusty; I awoke with the early sun and finished packing my saddlebags. Knowing how I love potatoes, Sema cooked some during breakfast for me to take as a picnic.

Keyif arrived having cast a hind shoe on the way, so my first task was to find a blacksmith in the back streets and we took our place in line behind a horse and cart. During shoeing my horse was relatively well-behaved, although it was necessary for people to twist his ears and mutter soothing noises. I had both his back feet re-shod, for balance, because the nail heads stuck out about a centimetre below the shoe. Turkish horse-shoes are solid plates with only a small hole for ventilation. It seemed to me that the inner space would easily fill with wet mud and cause problems of footrot, but the local horses all used them, so I would have to see how they worked out. The blacksmith also put a couple of new nails in each front shoe to give them extra grip.

I rode south through the sprawling city, stopping at a market to buy some tomato and *bastirma* (local meat cured in garlic and pepper) to go with Sema's potatoes. Keyif stopped every time he saw another horse, to paw the road and neigh aggressively.

We climbed up through mountains for two hours. It was steep but not arduous because the horse moved eagerly at a fast swinging walk. The road was dusty but not stony, and the only vehicle to pass us was a tractor pulling a cart, it was going just marginally faster than Keyif. In the cart was a family of nomads, sheltering from the hot sun under black umbrellas. They all waved and called greetings.

Later we passed some stone crofts beside another stream and stopped at its source for a lunchbreak. Keyif shared my picnic since, despite the spring, there wasn't much grass. It had been eaten by small brown marmots which, when they got used to us, came out of their burrows and scurried around.

Also feeling active, I began combing Keyif's mane and tail,

slow work and I doubted they had ever been groomed in his life; I made no impact on his tail, but his mane looked great.

Then just as I was about to saddle up, he lay down and rolled in the mud beside the spring. Wet and filthy, I had to wait for him to dry off since to saddle a wet horse is asking for saddle-sores. Actually he had one already, which I'd not noticed because I'd never seen him without a saddle. Stupid of me. When buying a horse one really should check everything. But I always forget something. The sore wasn't bad, it was partly healed and looked all right.

From there we branched off on to an overgrown track which led steeper and more directly up the mountains and by 4 p.m. we had reached the level of some old snow drifts; I walked up beside a large bank of snow and washed my face in the glacial stream which issued from it.

I lost the track in the snow but could see it snaking up the mountains above so we went cross-country following instinct. Short cropped turf made easy walking, and often I dismounted to stroll beside Keyif and rest his back. Soon we were looking down on the summer tents of pasturalists, dotted on the mountains' shoulders. Icy tarns provided water for them and their herds of black sheep.

It was like being part of the sky more than the land, in hot sun with chilly winds, seemingly we could go no higher. We passed an unexcavated square fortress, its outline showing through the turf, and part of its stone ramparts still exposed. Snowdrifts were heaped against the walls. On another mountain summit I could make out a larger fortress also covered by turf with one exposed wall. I wanted to absorb it all, though the haze blotted out the clarity beyond the cries of a hunting bird wheeling in wind currents above purple rock and green turf.

From time to time we rejoined the old track whose route was visible for miles as it crossed the mountain highlands. We passed several World War II machine-gun emplacements which, together with the forts, testify to Turkish strategic importance throughout the ages. This part of Turkey has been attacked by the Sumerians, Urartians, Cimmerians, Babylonians, Scythians, Medes, Persians, Romans, Byzantines, Arabs, Seljuks, Mongols, and that only gets us to the thirteenth century. Cyrus conquered this land, as did Alexander the Great, and in 36 BC Mark Antony's army wintered here, losing 24,000 men mostly through starvation and sickness after their local allies went home for the winter.

Some hillsides we loped across were covered in a haze of blue flowers. The mountain rock paled to white, with purple-flowering groundcover, then turned meadowlike with daisies, dandelions and buttercups. Keyif was still fresh and he broke into a triple whenever the ground was flat enough for speed. He was a pacer and he moved at a triple instead of a trot; the difference between Keyif and Shanaza, the black pacer of the Assassins' Valley, was that Shanaza was taught to pace, while Keyif did it naturally. He didn't know how to trot, but his pacing could be ambling or swift. He chose the speed and I chose the direction, still heading south cross-country and on the old road.

As the sun sank lower we came to a river where a track led away, presumably to a village. We followed it and soon I spotted a hamlet of stone cottages. Some young girls on the track didn't return my greeting, they looked at me in horror and then fled.

The hamlet had seemed almost deserted but within seconds of my arrival I was surrounded by scores of people who all stood and stared in silence. I introduced myself and asked if I could put the horse in one of their animal pens. The pens were enclosed by thorn fences with wide gaps, so I tethered him for extra security. He rushed around neighing; I sat nearby and tried to get to know the people. They told me their village's name was Hasan Aga Köyü; the men all came to shake hands, but the women didn't take my hand, they reached out and felt my breasts.

It was a bit disconcerting; I just smiled and took their hands off me and gave a handshake instead, but it happened so many times I wondered how I was expected to react. In mock indignation I touched one woman's chest in return but she only laughed. The women were wearing several layers of clothes despite the heat, and on their heads muslin shawls with em-broidered edges, and black silken tassels showing underneath. The front tassels were short like a fringe and the back tassels long to mid-back. The children, hordes of them, pressed around us tightly and whenever I got up to walk around they all followed. Occasionally the men chased them away with sticks, but they soon came back.

Keyif was restless, stamping and whinnying. One of his problems was a plague of tiny ants that kept crawling up on to his back, attacking his partly healed sore and biting it raw. The villagers didn't have any ointment for it so in the end I took my tube of toothpaste and made a ring of toothpaste around the sore, as a barricade against the ants.

Later I managed to find an empty stable for him to sleep in. I stayed with a family and after supper we all slept on floor mattresses with thick wool quilts. The night was hot and the room stuffy because the windows were closed against mosquitoes. But mosquitoes were plentiful inside and I had to pull the quilt up to my chin to stop them biting. My skin felt slimy with sweat and I dreamt that my bed was full of ants. In fact it was, and I kept rolling over to try and squash them.

In the morning the people wouldn't let me leave before a breakfast of hot bread and fresh *mast*, and because they would not accept any payment, I took some family photographs to send back to them. In really remote villages like this one, money is not often of immediate practical value and to repay hospitality I always have a supply of things like lighters for the men or headscarves and earrings from Shepherd's Bush market for the women. It may sound a bit neo-colonial, but it gives immediate pleasure and is a clear way of saying thank you.

So I saddled Keyif and we made tracks over the hills and back to the dirt road which would lead me to Tekman village. The morning air felt good, I hoped that sometime during the day I'd find a secluded river to bathe in, but meantime Keyif was fresh and we covered miles at an eager triple.

We climbed up a series of hills and slowly down into a valley where I could see a village. My map was hopelessly small-scale so I'd begun compiling a home-made version, from the directions of local people; this suggested the village would be Katran Koyu, which was confirmed by an old man carrying firewood along the road. He said there was a short-cut over the mountains to Tekman, but insisted that I stop for tea at his house on the way.

His house was at the end of the village, a stone cottage with low tunnel entrance and several rooms whose floors and walls were covered in rich red and blue Turkish carpets, with cushions surrounding the walls as backrests. Many other people came to tea, or just to sit and look. A few of the women reached out and grabbed my chest and then described it to the menfolk, but mostly they were content to sit and look and smile. My Turkish vocabulary was small but increasing daily. The two most useful words in the dictionary are *tamam* for 'yes/that's right' and *yok*, an all-purpose negative. To say no, Turks, like Greeks, raise their eyes and nod their head backwards.

When I felt that Keyif had rested and eaten enough hay, we moved on, taking the short cut which led up into undulating mountains. It was a glorious day of sun and wind; beautiful open scenery with outcrops of red jagged rock; the path visible as a dent in meadowlands of grass and wild flowers. Keyif was being a joy to ride, he needed no urging, running more often than walking; I rode with slack reins and hadn't yet touched him with my heels; only needing to say '*Yavaş*' (slow down) or '*Haydi gidelim*' (Let's go) for a faster pace, and all his paces were extremely comfortable. My saddlebags were strapped down well enough so they didn't flap around even when we cantered. From the hilltop we began a long descent to the Araxes River which flows past Tekman, and much later marks the Russian border.

Tekman is a big village, we passed a salt-making project whose pools of salty water were evaporating in the sun to leave mounds of glittering crystals, and we reached a tributary of the Araxes. The water looked too deep to ford and the bridge too rickety for a horse. I opted for wading, pulled the saddlebags as high as I could and chose a point which seemed likely to have a submerged sandbar. We only got a slight wetting.

In Tekman we found a public stable and the owner took me in also, giving me lunch of bread and cheese in his house. The Prime Minister of Turkey, Kenan Evran, was due to visit Tekman that afternoon to look at the agriculture and salt-making, so I asked if the village girls were planning to dance in his honour. They said no, but found the idea so appealing they began to dance for me: with arms outstretched, shoulders shivering rapidly, and fingers clicking, not in the western way but using both hands to click index against second fingers. There was no music so we improvised with our voices in chorus while a girl sang a solo. It was a shame that Kenan Evran couldn't see them. I would have liked to meet him but it would have meant waiting about two hours and I didn't really want to attract any official attention.

It had occurred to me that I didn't have permission from the authorities to make my ride, though I didn't consider that it was necessary; an official who allows a project may become responsible for it; why ask someone else to accept liability for a journey? As a traveller I have to be responsible for what happens. This is one of the early lessons in the stages of travelling. The tourist office offers Eastern Turkey as a land of adventure, and that was precisely what I was going to have, a long good one.

So we left during Prime Minister Evran's arrival, as unobtrusively as possible. We recrossed the tributary, went up over a ridge of hills and waded through the great Araxes River on a southward bend; then slowly up into an empty range of hills on a small dirt track with not a shred of traffic. I didn't see a village all afternoon and wondered if we would be camping out that night. The basic problem with camping was that I had to be sure I wasn't found, since men seeing a camp were likely to make a nocturnal visit and my main fear was of losing Keyif, for there were no trees to conceal a horse and camp.

Later I saw men on the hillsides cutting hay, their horses grazing free. Keyif pranced along at the sight of mares and foals. We cantered over to one group of men and asked about villages, they said there was one called Gümüslü about five hills away. The path followed the contours so we made good speed, although we must have covered fifty kilometres already that day. The late afternoon sun's slanting rays bathed the land in a golden light.

In a wide valley with a stream that meandered continually looping back on itself, I saw flocks of wild ducks; the air was full of the humming of bees, small wonder in a valley so lush with snapdragons, yellow cowslips, deep blue forget-me-nots and more I could not name, wild roses in purple, pink, mauve, yellow and scarlet. The rocks were covered with red lichen that the local people used as a type of henna. From the reeds of the stream came the warbling of frog song. We reached an area of basalt rock which had split naturally into square pillars and was being locally extracted, and shortly afterwards I saw the track leading to Gümüslü, an old stone village set in a gulley among trees. As I approached I met a friendly young courting couple who took me to their family home and invited me to stay. Their stable was a lower room inside the house, and the animals, including Keyif, walked in through the front door.

Keyif and I entered a scene of celebration. There were people dancing to the music of traditional guitars. The family was celebrating a *sunnet* or circumcision ceremony. Two boys aged four and six had just been circumcised and the family proudly showed me their bandaged cuts. The doctor was an uncle. Gathered at the house were twenty-seven members of the family, some having come a long distance for this event. The parents were delightful, as were their grown children and the courting couple, Sonar and Gul, who I'd met on the way. One uncle had brought whisky and several men were as merry as grigs. The family room was carpeted with several layers of carpet and, as in Katran Koyu, cushions were backed up around the walls, which were themselves hung with other carpets. Light came from a couple of pressure lamps.

When I listened to conversations I realised that many villagers were not speaking Turkish, their language was Zazaca, an old dialect. They said this village had been here since Byzantine times. Some had now intermarried with Kurds. We feasted on beef and stuffed peppers with sheep's yoghurt, served in the usual Turkish way on a big round tray which everyone could reach while sitting around it crosslegged on the floor, helping themselves by using their hands to wrap pieces of bread around each mouthful of food.

Afterwards when I was offered a bath I accepted with pleasure, still sticky from the previous night's heat and dusty from the day's ride. The women took me into the kitchen, a dark smoky room with black rafters; they sat me in a shallow tin tub, poured jugs of hot water over me and scrubbed my skin until it tingled.

We all slept in the family room on floor mattresses; mosquitoes were few, or at any rate I was too soundly asleep to notice. At 5 a.m. I awoke because cats were fighting outside, ducks were quacking, people calling, and my horse neighing in the room below me. I took him out and tried tethering him to graze on the hill but he rushed around senselessly whinnying to other horses, so I brought him back indoors and gave him an armful of freshly cut hay.

My breakfast was sheep's cheese mixed with nut oil *lore*, and locally made jam on fresh bread. Afterwards the young man called Sonar and I wandered around the village watching smoke rising from earthen roofs in the early sun. In contrast to what I'd seen before, the stone cottages here were made of odd-sized stones, roughly squared and held in mud mortar, with flat roofs of timber and earth that bounced slightly when we walked on them.

Brightly-clad girls were herding black sheep, while big shaggy dogs yawned and stretched, and women carrying pairs of buckets on a shoulder-yoke ambled down to the village pump for water. One woman with a spindle was winding wool for socks; others were beating wodges of wool for making new mattresses. Sonar said it took ten sheep's fleeces to make a quilt, and twenty to fill a mattress. People greeted me in a friendly way and we stopped for tea with a Kurdish-Zazaca family. The wife wore a necklace of solid gold coins. Most of the women have embroidered the edges of their yashmaks with macramé beadwork. They told me that my visit was the first time a foreigner had been to their village.

Sonar explained that this was a former bandit village, and his grandfather had been notorious; as I understood it he had killed sixty-three people. The family pressed me not to leave. 'Why not stay a day and join in a picnic outing?' So I stayed but the picnic got mysterious because at noon lunch was served in the house, a special feast for *sunnet* with dishes of liver and kidneys, good iron for the circumcised boys. Then later a truck arrived and the family scrambled into it, fourteen children in the open back, some older people in the cab, and six of us middle generation squashed together sitting on the cab's roof. Precarious but with a spectacular view.

We drove a few kilometres back up the main valley and stopped at some beehives to get honey, then climbed on foot into the hills. A spring of very cold mountain water was our first goal, and on up to the site of a former Armenian village, almost indiscernible now, but the family knew the location of several houses, fireplaces and graves, even the graves of children. The Christian population had been massacred by invading Moslems about 1,200 years ago, but according to Sonar the Armenians had been evil and got what they deserved.

So this was part of Armenia, which I'd first seen on a map drawn by Ptolemy, stretching from the Black Sea Alps to Mesopotamia, Georgia and Azerbaijan bordering north to east, a plateau at a height of 1,300-1,800 metres which included the Lake Van basin. Military fatigue and religious segmentation had given the Arabs the chance to invade Armenia. The Greeks tried to re-occupy the kingdom but its inhabitants preferred Arab rule to the oppressive Greek taxes. Armenian independent-mindedness clashed with its Arab overlords, and in the eighth century the Arab viceroy was reported to have ordered the killing of Armenian high nobility. But that was nothing to the genocide that came later. In the meantime the Greeks re-conquered Armenia, and many of the population emigrated.

A few kilometres away we walked up to a tall hill of weirdly scoured rocks and fox holes. On the peak was the ruin of Hasbek fortress, a Greek stronghold. I could see where treasure seekers have been digging in the foundations, and Sonar said they found various bits of gold jewellery and coins. I found glazed red pottery fragments. Four valleys radiated from this fortress hill, with meandering streams in lush flower-filled valleys. Between them the barley fields were being ruffled by the wind, rippling through in feathery waves. On the summit the wind tore at my hair. On a nearby crag we could make out the remains of another fortress, and far to the south I could see a snowy mountain range which Sonar's father, Yusuf, said marked my route for the next day; my next destination, Hinis, being on the plain beyond.

As for the picnic, we munched peeled thornbush stems and tangy peeled sorrel stems; I think picnic means outing. Turning a large truck around on a single lane dirt road proved problematical! But all things come to those who persevere and within an hour we were motoring back, clinging on to the cab roof for dear life.

In the evening we were all invited out to an uncle's cottage. He had killed a sheep and, after hanging some strips of mutton out to dry on the line, we went inside for the feast. One can tell the family pecking order by watching who takes the best seats and who rises to give up their cushions to whom. It's done with respect, not grudgingly; adherence to this order of seniority is a way of handling all social situations, so that everyone knows their place in the group.

When discussing my onward journey the men warned me I would be crossing bandit country, and to be especially careful in the Hinis region. Sonar said that whatever happened, I must not stop near Hinis, and an uncle gave me two notes of introduction to some friends ahead.

The walk back from the cottage was very starry, no moon yet, we could hardly see the narrow log bridge to the house. Back inside there was a surprise announcement, of the betrothal of Sonar and Gul. They had known each other since childhood; he was now twenty-one, she twenty. Gul went around the room kissing the hands and both cheeks of some women and men, then Sonar did the same to the other people. Gul's father, Mustapha, put two rings on her hands, the important one being the gold filigree band on her right hand. On her left hand he put a gold and ruby ring, and round her neck he fastened a gold pendant. Everyone in the room began laughing and kissing each other, and some were crying tears of emotion. In a year's time the couple would marry; I wished them happiness from the bottom of my heart.

14   Over the hills to Lake Van

So Keyif and I set our heads towards the snow-capped mountain range I had seen from the fortress hilltop. At one point he wouldn't go past some women washing wool, because he was afraid of the long poles they were using to beat the wool clean in the water. But they scuttled for safety when he plunged around, and we got past. Up again into higher mountains, the track was now just a four-wheel drive type, and when we reached that summit we seemed to be higher than the snowy range ahead. On our peak was a tall black stone obelisk, ancient and weatherworn. Skylarks sang and hovered in the air.

The track led to a rolling plateau, I saw some women on horseback, two riding tandem on a stallion that jerked its head up in response to Keyif's shrill whinny. At Hairon village we descended steeply to cross a rushing river, then sharply up into the mountains. The state of the track made me wonder how it deserved to be classified as a road, and it reminded me of one I'd ridden along in Africa. When I had asked incredulously if cars ever used that road, the reply had been, 'Oh yes, plenty, there was one in 1964!'

Now we arrived on top of another plateau, grassy and smooth enough to gallop. Snow patches lay around. This is Bingol Mountain, also known as 'the mountain of a thousand tarns' and 'the cauldron of a thousand pools'. The Araxes river rises from them.

After about five kilometres on Bingol Mountain we met a nomad woman on an old white mare. Her four children accompanied her, one in front of the saddle, one behind, and two walking. She told me I was on the wrong route for Hinis and I should come with her to her *yaila* or summer camp. Keyif was inclined to follow the old mare, and I was quite happy to follow her mistress.

The route left the path and took off cross-country, fording streams, going around beautiful blue lakes, and up and down craggy climbs. At one which was too rough for the safety of the second infant sitting behind her in the saddle, she set the toddler on the ground, to be led along by its brother. They had a hard time clambering over the big rocks so I offered to take the infant up in front on my saddle, to which they agreed with alacrity.

He was fairly safe because I could hold him as well as the reins, and Keyif was very surefooted. But I was terrified of dropping the child when we came to streams that had to be jumped. Firmly clasping him and the horse's mane I urged Keyif forward at a canter. He jumped cleanly. More rocky tors, the miles passed, and the infant fell asleep. Finally, almost invisible against the rocky background, I saw a camp of tents and makeshift rock-shelters.

We were welcomed with cups of tea, and I tethered Keyif to rest in a rock pen, but he was restless, neighing at the white mare and the other horses. The *yaila* was made up of thirty-five tents and rock shelters, for 140 people, mostly women and children. The women did the usual boob-feel and it suddenly occurred to me that perhaps they were just checking I really was a woman, because they would never have encountered a solitary foreign woman travelling as I was, dressed as a man in trousers and shirt, my long hair caught up inside a man's cap.

The inside of the shelters was not high enough for me to stand upright, but they were quite roomy. We drank tea in a tent which rocked in the strong gusting wind. They use these shelters every year for two to three months after the main snows have melted. Mostly women come because their men are working in their home villages to harvest hay. Children come to tend the flocks, and the women's work is to milk the sheep, goats and cattle every day, and churn the milk into yoghurt and cheese. On the flat roofs of the shelters were plants which are used to kindle fires. One ground-shrub here is exceptionally flammable and will burn even when green. The summit behind the camp was still snow-coated, and the wind had a pleasantly icy chill. We were probably at 3,000 metres, with the summit behind the camp nearly 500 metres higher. Halfway through my tea there was a commotion outside and cries of 'Your horse has broken free!'

I dashed outside in time to see Keyif galloping away across the mountain. I had visions of him running all the way back to Erzurum. Ten people joined me in pursuit of him, we raced across the mountainside, spaced out to give us a better chance of catching him. He caused havoc amongst a herd of horses, but we managed to head him back towards the camp where he stampeded in among the tents. Frightened women waved their arms and screeched at him, which only made matters worse.

Someone managed to catch the old white mare and rode her around near Keyif. Thank goodness for that old white mare; Keyif made whinnies of affection, and calmed down, although it still took us half an hour more to catch him, using the mare as a shield, me on foot hiding behind her shoulder and trying to walk her within reach of his trailing rope.

Finally successful, I tethered him very securely near the mare and went to finish my tea. Then I stayed for lunch of fresh yoghurt, bread and cheese, and watched women milking sheep and goats. The camp was guarded by big Anatolian dogs, I met one ambling along with a dead sheep's head in its mouth. It was a peaceful place but for the howling wind.

When I left to follow the right way to Hinis, I got lost in the mountains again. I had thought my route should go over the mountain and down to the plain, and this was my error. But it was too wild and beautiful with the myriad blue lakes and the crags for me to worry about being lost, and every now and then I caught sight of other *yailas* or heard the calls of herdsboys as they shouted to each other with voices that echoed across the desolation.

Deciding that I'd gone in a circle I tried to find the original *yaila*, but to reach Bingol's main peak was not straightforward, the rocks were more suited to a goat than to a horse, and the *yaila* was so well camouflaged that I didn't spot it until quite close. This time the son of my original escort volunteered to show me a short cut to the Hinis track. The path took me back down to a village I'd passed before, where I'd taken the wrong route. However now I could see the Hinis road, earlier hidden by the slope of another mountain.

Coming out of the village Keyif called to two horses. In response they came galloping over, and closed in to attack. I shouldn't have been surprised, since stallions often fight other strange stallions on their territory. But almost too late I saw the larger horse rear up above me and begin striking out with his forelegs. Fortunately I had the long end of Keyif's halter rope in my hand, so I swung it in rapid circles. The knotted end caught the attacking stallion on the nose, he snorted and wheeling away, kicked savagely out with his hind hooves. But they missed us, as did the other horse's kicks. I kept whirling the rope and the stallions gave us room to pass.

The dirt road hugged a ledge as it descended the steeply winding valley. An old man was trudging along the road, lost in thought, and I wondered if we would be able to pass him without him realising I was a foreigner. He paid no heed to the horse's steps but as we passed he glanced up and gave such a grunt of surprise that he tripped over. He recovered his dignity and I tried to keep the laugh off my face.

A few kilometres later as we walked through a hamlet some large dogs hurtled over, snarling and leaping up at me. I drew my knees up to the top of the saddle but it was hard to keep my balance with Keyif dancing nervously. 'Don't panic,' I told him, 'it's me they want to kill, not you.' Indeed they only had a small try at biting his legs, perhaps they knew they would get kicked, and it wasn't their job to bite horses. But they leapt up towards me with yellow fangs bared. We tried to outrun them but they ran circles around us, so I pulled Keyif back to a walk, acting unconcerned, and hoping we would soon reach the limit of their territory. They chased us for about three kilometres before going back. Two attacks in one day, I hoped the people weren't going to do the same, and I remembered Sonar's warning, 'Don't stop *anywhere* on the way to Hinis.'

We continued at a fast pace downhill along the valleyside, among tumbled boulders and stunted oak trees. Partridges were pecking among their low branches. Three hours later the sun was almost ready to set and a farmer told me that Hinis was still two hours away. Obviously we were not going to reach our intended 'safe house'.

So I stopped at a village and went to see the *muhtar*, or headman. It was a prosperous-looking village, I hoped from hard work not ill-gotten gains. The *muhtar* was very hospitable, Keyif was led away to his stable, and I stopped worrying when the *muhtar* said that any robbers and horse-thieves would be shot. The *muhtar*'s nine brothers and six sisters included Nurse Rahime, who patrols on horseback. During the evening she explained how she takes her clinic up to the *yailas* to tend the sick.

The household was up at 5 a.m. and after breakfast of bread and cheese I rode on down the valley. Several valleys joined and looking down one I could see Hinis town, still at least ten kilometres away. Actually I managed to detour around the town and didn't stop there.

Our road switchbacked over the hills in a straight line, and by the turning for Karaçoban we stopped at a gas station; tea for me and a half-hour rest for Keyif but the flies tormented him dreadfully. I had found a tube of insect repellent in my luggage so I smeared it on him. But he needed gallons. Shortly after leaving there we came to a stream and stopped for Keyif to drink, and before I realised what was happening he started to lie down in it. Not that I blamed him, the cool water would be soothing to all those bites, but it couldn't be allowed since he would have rolled on the baggage – so I yelled and kicked him until he got the message.

Next I looked for a village where he could take his midday rest in a stable, which is cooler and relatively fly-free; by now I'd given up on Sonar's warnings about bandits and bad people, relying on my common sense. When I was hailed by unsavoury men I just waved back and didn't stop. But there was nothing to fear, people were generally wonderful to me. At the village of Belitaş I asked a man if there was a stable my horse could use until the heat of the day had passed, and he immediately understood; he took me to his cottage, put Keyif in a stable with five calves and numerous ducklings, and invited me into an adjoining room for refreshment. We sat on cushions on a raised platform, and in a corner kitchen area his wife made tea followed by lunch of bread and a meat-tomato dish.

One by one, many women wearing yashmaks came to see me, children's faces appeared in the chimney hole above us, and much dust began to fall. Like most cottages here, the roofs were slightly domed with a central hole and wickerwork chimney stack. The women brought me a yashmak to wear, they were appalled by my manly cap and insisted on my learning to wrap the yashmak properly around my head – which involved letting the decorative beaded fringe hang over the forehead, while one end of the scarf came over the mouth and nose and wrapped back to the crown of the head, giving maximum effect to the beaded edges. The nose-mouth bit could be pulled down to eat or drink. Each style of scarf seems to have a different name; a *tulbend* is a headscarf, though if it's closed it's a *yashmak*, and if it's embroidered it's *oya*. The closed over-wrapper is a *buruk*, and the brown body-cover, which I'd seen often in Erzurum, is an *ehram*. I pointed out that mine wouldn't shield my face from the sun, so one woman pulled the brow forward into a peak.

The women's faces were big and slightly heavy-looking but at the same time they were comely, good-natured faces with clear honest wide-set eyes. They seemed to have an average of eight children each. The man of the house, Ali, was a farmer but his herds were currently up at a *yaila*. While saddling to leave I noticed a lovely old ox-cart with solid wooden wheels. Ali said it would be pulled up to the *yaila* later in the week.

The road that afternoon was dull, flat and stony, following a broad valley cultivated with beans, potatoes, tomatoes, barley, and hay which people were harvesting and raking with long wooden-pegged rakes. Other disc-wheeled ox carts were in use; the ancestors of the Armenians had carts like these back in the Bronze Age. Chariots with solid wheels were used here by the Sumerians in about 2500 BC.

Occasionally the road crossed a river that both Keyif and I longed to swim in. The day was hotter than any so far. We were heading for Karaçoban where I'd been given a note to another 'safe house'; I could see the village at the end of the plain, a long straggling stone village with narrow lanes and many teashops where old men would be sitting discussing local matters. According to my dictionary, *'çoban'* means shepherd, and *'kara'* means black or gloomy.

For me it took on a gloomy hue because the man to whom the note was addressed was away, and his wife wasn't understanding. A crowd gathered, they read her the note and said of course I should stay, they gave me *ayran*, a yoghurt drink, and asked what my horse would eat. I replied plenty of hay and offered to pay for it. No, as a friend I couldn't pay, the hay would come soon. But soon it would be dark and no hay had arrived. I could see the track I would take on the morrow, leading up into mountains where the outline of a distant Byzantine fortress stood out against the mauve evening sky. Zirnak Kale, it would be on my route. And I watched the narrow sliver of the new moon rise.

Dusk became night, still no hay, and when finally I asked what time it would arrive they said tomorrow morning. It upset me that a horse-using community would leave a hungry horse all night without food, but so often in villages it had already happened that no one fed him until I insisted, so again I had to insist on finding hay. Conversation was difficult since people's first language was Kurdish, though a few men could speak German, having worked some years in German factories.

A tiny old lady joined us, wearing a yellow shirt, red jerkin, green sleeves, purple cuff-covers, a blue floral skirt held up by numerous bands and a black apron at front and back, with pink socks and plastic sandals. Later in the privacy of the cottage the women showed me that they wore five layers of skirts and cotton undertrousers, and five layers of tops; I asked if it didn't make them feel hot and they said no, not at all. Hum! Perhaps they wear it all like a status symbol, proving how many clothes they own. One of the women was mother of sixteen children, while another had fourteen. Our supper was a meagre bowl of stewed tomatoes and bread. The family was obviously not poor but perhaps the best was reserved for the men.

My wake-up call was provided at 5 a.m. when a kitten playing in the rafters dislodged a mass of rubble on to me. An early start and only fifty kilometres to cover today; yesterday we did over sixty. After crossing the river our track wound up and over two mountain ranges. No wild flowers, only dry grass and the loud chirring of cicadas. In a lonely spot we met three unpleasant-looking men on horseback, they eyed my saddle-bags and asked me to give them cigarettes or money, but fortunately they were going the opposite direction so I kept a fast pace until they were gone from sight. The morning became blazing hot, and noticing a stream I guided Keyif down to it, but the water was salty, which showed in the white crusty layer along its edges. A second stream was also salty.

We were being troubled by flies and had also attracted several bees. Suddenly a swarm of at least fifty bees surrounded us. They bit both me and Keyif, not stinging, they were biting for blood. I began to feel a little desperate and on seeing a herd of goats I rode through them, hoping to lose the bees among the goats. Quite successful. After twenty kilometres the track led out of the mountains and down on to a plain where the heat intensified. There were two villages, one where some boys threw stones at my horse, until I lost my temper and yelled so angrily it stopped the boys in their tracks. At the second village I asked an elderly man if he had a stable, and he immediately called his wife to expect a guest and a horse.

After meeting the menfolk and drinking *ayran*, the men left and the young women took over. They turned the radio to Turkish music, full blast, lit cigarettes, took off their yashmaks, and began to dance: hip flicking, finger clicking, moving round each other and shaking their shoulders. They insisted that I dance too, and teach them a Western dance. One woman stood by the window as lookout, and when she saw the father approaching they quickly turned off the radio and put on their yashmaks again.

One of the girls was engaged to marry a man in Karaçoban; she asked me if I had liked the place, so I warned her that she would probably have to wear five layers of skirts. Here they were just wearing cotton trousers under one skirt. Since the day was so hot I took a long midday break and gave myself the luxury of an hour's nap, which the family had suggested, but it's quite hard to fall asleep with twenty people staring at every twitch. So I pulled my yashmak over my face, but every few minutes the girls would lift it up to see if I was still awake.

Before leaving I asked if anything could be done to prevent the bees biting; the old man said they would be bad until the day grew cooler and he gave me a leafy twig to use as a fly switch. We left at 4 p.m. and the bees were still atrocious, about sixty swarmed continually around us. I wondered if they were attracted by the noise of Keyif's hooves on the hard-baked earth, because bees are known to swarm to sharp noises. Other types of flies were also plentiful including ones that whined around my head and flew into my ears. Apart from all that, I thought I had caught fleas because my legs and stomach were covered in red bites that itched. Not amusing.

The land was dull typical Anatolian-type plateau, cultivated with vast areas of wheat and barley. The long straight road led to the Murat river, which flows to Elazig Lake. With the evening cool the flies and bees went away so I kept riding. Far to the south-east was the majestic cone of Süphan Dağ, 4,850 metres.

It was long past sunset when we reached the town of Bulanik and I wondered if I had been unwise to think of spending a night in a town since horse stables were few. But chance led me to a delightful family. Keyif was catered for, and I was bathed, scrubbed, dried and fed. Unfortunately I discovered that I had lost my dictionary, and also mislaid my sunglasses.

I wanted to have a lie-in next morning, but soon after dawn I had to get up because I could see a goose trying to swallow my shoelaces. For the morning's ride I was plagued by tiny gnats so I resorted to wearing full yashmak. Once clear of that plain things improved but I was fed up because our route lay along an asphalt road with traffic which we both hated, and also the nails in Keyif's shoes had worn down almost flat which made his feet slip too easily for speed. In exasperation I turned east down a tractor track, on the theory that it would have to bisect any smaller road heading to Lake Van.

My frustration evaporated as the sandy path led through rolling hills and across streams. One tree in the whole landscape, I rested beneath it while Keyif rolled in the stream. In the village where we stopped at noon I was the property of the men and many people came to say hello to the first tourist to visit their village. One man asked if he could buy Keyif, and when I refused he nodded saying Keyif was a good horse.

Children were occupied with plaiting ropes of green hay; and two cockerels were fighting, closing in with ripping talons and almost immediately parting to cluck insults at each other. Some women arrived and I let them bath me, and wash my clothes as well in the hope of killing the fleas. But it occurred to me that perhaps they weren't fleas, they could have been harvest bugs, very likely with all this scything going on and me carrying hay around.

The women also took me into the kitchen and taught me to make local bread, flipping the round balls of dough from hand to hand until it became a large thin oval which was then slapped on the side of the underground clay oven. The heat was fearsome, I didn't envy the women this daily chore even though I love fresh hot bread. For lunch we had a delicious mixture of sheep's cheese and a dish of stewed fruit – I wanted to ask its name but without a dictionary it would have been meaningless, so I asked anyway and was delighted when he pointed to the dish and said 'My name is Eric' – it took me back to my arrival in Turkey two and a half months previously, in Ürgüp bazaar when I'd first been introduced to Turkish plums.

The afternoon was lovely, cantering on soft paths over a gently undulating plain. Low mountains on every horizon gave a sense of an unseen beyond. The canyons which cut down below ground level were equally unseen until we reached their edges. Late afternoon we came to a road and turned left on to it, but resentfully since it was stony and Keyif slowed to a crawl. He was probably growing tired, we'd had three days of good mileage since he had that day of rest at Sonar's village, and I resolved to rest and feed him more. He should have been eating five kilos of hay three times a day, because there was no better fodder available at this time of year. He was no thinner than when we began our journey but he was slowing down and now I needed to use my heels and voice occasionally.

At sunset there was no sign of a village and when I detoured to a haycart the men said the next village was fifteen kilometres away, I should go west to a village only four kilometres distant. This I did, taking a direct line over the hills and, although it grew dark, I could see the village, and saw a boy set out to meet me on another horse. He was the *muhtar's* son, come to guide me in.

The *muhtar*, Teksi, was a kind and hospitable host and his house was soon crowded with his family and friends. The evening talk was of the gold that men had found in the hills, and one showed me his collection of coins, most had Arabic script while one battered coin had an eagle emblem.

The following day I made an early start and didn't try to follow the road, I had located my compass in my luggage and used it to keep a south-east course. According to the map there would be another lake before Lake Van called Lake Nazik. We were crossing a pass into the great Van Basin. The plain narrowed into a funnel-shaped valley between mountain ranges. Boulder-fields made our progress a little difficult, and the wildlife on the plain included a number of tortoises. I saw five that morning, the largest almost half a metre long.

At Ari village we joined a track which led south into the mountains, but the track petered out in the grass so we continued straight towards the neck. Reaching its crest I looked down into the valley that holds Nazik Lake, sparkling and blue.

We hurried to the shore and at a lush patch of clover I unsaddled Keyif to graze. He flattened the clover, rolling on it non-stop until he was dark brown with mud. We made our proper noontime stop at the lakeside village of Dilburnu, where its natural charm, combined with the headman's kindness, persuaded me to stop there for the rest of the day. First of all Keyif and I went for a swim, me fully dressed, as propriety demands, although the men swim in trunks.

The waves lapping against the sand made Keyif snort with mistrust but the sight of so much water won the day and he waded in. The bottom shelved slowly and it took a couple of minutes to lead him out of his depth. Yet he swam strongly and enjoyed it enough to return for more. Offshore was a small island which once had a fort, and I could see the remains of an ancient road on the isthmus leading to the island.

Later in the day many people went fishing in the lake; it is freshwater and the *muhtar*, Zakin, said they catch various fish. One is a type of flatfish reaching a weight of twenty-five kilos. Pelicans also come here to catch fish. Zakin added that theirs is a lucky and abundant village, and this year he had instigated a collection to help the poor and needy peoples of Africa. He showed me their letter of thanks.

In the evening I sat out among the women, watching their big homely faces as they worked at rope-making from long grasses, feeding in more grasses when the rope thinned, twisting it, doubling, winding and redoubling, and their children helped by twisting it on hand rollers. Other women were making yarn for *kilims*, from combed out sheep's wool. They laughed at my efforts to spin yarn.

The village originally had a wall around it, with a fortress and two gates, but now only a small fragment of the wall is left where it meets the lake. I liked the way that each time I took Keyif down to the lake for a drink, the colours of the water had changed, reflecting the sky, and Süphan Dağ with its streaks of dark volcanic rock showing through the ice and snow, would appear and vanish. Many drinks were necessary because Keyif had been licking a salt-grinding stone, and I made a note to provide him with salt every day or so.

The following morning there was a strong wind blowing and the lake was rough with waves. I rode cross-country over the lakeshore hills, enjoying the panorama as we came down into the Van Basin. That lake was not yet visible, but I could see how Süphan Dağ which seemed to be across Nazik Lake, actually rose from down near Lake Van's shore. Seven kilometres further we passed through Ovakisla village where some ancient semi-underground dwellings were now being used as sheep pens. The sky was clear and cloudless, and then, beyond the horizon of spring flowers, I saw Lake Van spread out before me.

15   *Fabled shores*

We descended into the ancient lakeshore town of Ahlat, past old houses of rose-coloured stone set in gardens, and a few Seljuk tombs, large cylindrical buildings, like stubby rockets with conical roofs of stone slabs. On the edge of a ravine are vestiges of a once gigantic fortress wall. But it is the Seljuk tombs that are Ahlat's pride. One sat beside my road, a second was tucked away among leafy walnut-trees behind a house, and fifty metres down the road was a tomb with vestibule attached, open-sided containing a stone platform. Other tombs can be seen in vacant plots of ground around town, or half hidden in orchards, some are twelve-faced cylinders, or built on a square base with a pointed top, a few are ornate with attached rooms and blind arches. The style of Seljuk building was intended to express piety. Accommodation for me and horse was offered by a family living near two of the old tombs.

In the afternoon I made a shopping list and went in search of a blacksmith, but didn't find anything I was looking for, no dictionary or sunglasses, and although I found two blacksmiths, neither had any horseshoes. The search took me miles east of Ahlat, cantering along the deserted sandy beaches of Lake Van's shoreline, to a village where I was directed into a court-yard shaded by vines. An idyllic spot, men were making a new cart, still using solid wooden wheels, while the wood frame was held together by wooden pegs, no nails. Needless to say, no horseshoes either, but they gave Keyif a bowl of barley, quite a treat since this year's barley was not yet ready for harvest and last year's supply was long finished. Back in town I managed to procure some lucerne for him by dint of flagging down a passing truck. Beautiful hay, lucky horse.

The next day I rode west out of town through the Seljuk graveyard, with its elegant headstones two to three metres tall and decorated in lacy incised patterns and Arabic script. Lichen is growing over them and most are leaning at different angles among the weeds, stretching as a forest to the cliffs above the lake. It is a strange and beautiful place. Keyif swerved just in time to avoid treading on a tortoise.

We followed the cliffs of Lake Van, then down to the beach where we splashed along in the shallows, until reaching a military zone. On the sand were parked rows of armoured vehicles and field guns and between them marched soldiers; no one paid any attention to us, and we hurried because I wanted to get clear before the firing began. But at the far end of the artillery range we ran into trouble on the wrong side of a marshy lagoon. I tried to make Keyif cross a patch of dry marsh, he was suspicious but gave in to my insistence. Halfway across, the crust of the marsh collapsed and Keyif sank rapidly to his belly. His front feet sank first and I was thrown, or rather since I'd instinctively kicked my feet free of the stirrups I let myself fall, knowing that Keyif was better off without my weight to hinder him. Together we floundered out of the marsh and on to dry land, where I left him to graze while I unloaded and cleaned our baggage.

Clean again, I re-saddled Keyif and continued west along the beach. No sooner had I remounted than sudden explosive gunfire reverberated all around. Firing practice had begun. The noise was deafening and when a small aeroplane flew overhead they turned the anti-aircraft guns on it. I patted Keyif's neck and told him, 'Don't panic, they're only guns.'

The firing went on for about an hour, growing more distant as we raced away. At noon we stopped in a lakeside village for a swim. Lake Van is alkaline, sodium alkaline, the water feels silky, almost soapy, and it never freezes; the villagers wash their clothes simply by trailing them in the water, and since I was swimming fully dressed I felt well-cleaned. Drinking water is supplied by a canal from Nazik Lake. Van's water is not good for humans, animals or irrigation, though they do catch a type of herring which some women were eating for lunch. A horde of children accompanied me for the swim, many of them with hair bleached blond from frequent swimming in the lake.

My midday host had two wives, both young and pretty. He assured me they didn't fight, and added that he had paid £400 for the second wife three years ago. They both were wearing velvet dresses and told me their ages were fourteen and sixteen. I was continually surprised by how much older people looked than their age. A man brought in a sheaf of barley which all the men examined before agreeing it would be another ten days until the harvest. I was looking forward to that since Keyif could use the extra energy.

They also talked about the village's 500 cows and 5,000 sheep up at a *yaila* on Nemrut Dağ, twenty kilometres away, and said I should go there. The way in is usually closed by snow until July but was now clear. Accordingly I changed course and headed north-west up behind the village on to the lower slopes of Nemrut, a not-quite-extinct volcano.

The climb up to 3,300 metres was not difficult or very steep, though we stopped often because the wild grasses were tall and plentiful and I suspected that the land close to the *yaila* would be grazed bare.

As we climbed I could better understand the shape of Nemrut Dağ's enormous volcanic cone, it had blown its top right off leaving a crater several miles in circumference. From the rim we looked down into a jumble of solidified lava and rocks the volcano had been in the process of spewing.

The descent into the crater was steep and dusty, a fine pale ash puffing up in clouds under Keyif's hooves. The sun was setting and I hurried because the night would be cold unless I could find a *yaila*. The crater's cliffs glowed in the fading light.

Down on the volcano's floor we reached a lake and, following its shore, I saw a *yaila* of about twelve stone shelters and tents, full of activity as livestock came down from high pastures for the night. Cows were being milked, water was being fetched, fires were being kindled for cooking.

The women were friendly but weren't sure how to help me, they couldn't imagine that I'd want to stay with them. But after tethering Keyif they took me in, one group fed me, another offered me an empty shelter to sleep in, and before long they all wanted to sit and chat and make sure I wasn't a man.

The night was cold and I slept badly because Keyif outside kept whinnying at other horses and pulling hard at his tether which shook the rocks my shelter was built from. I awoke before dawn and lay waiting for enough light to streak the sky before I could get up.

Everyone was up at dawn, milking cattle, fetching water, and brewing tea. My breakfast was flat bread smothered in the skin of a delicious creamy *mast*. Gallons of *mast* were being used for making cheese. When I saddled Keyif we went off to explore more of the hills and lakes and smoke-holes of the crater's interior.

From the southern rim I found a disused track running along a contour of Nemrut Dağ for miles, high up overlooking Van Lake. Far below I could see the town of Tatvan, beyond which coves and headlands vanished into the distance. Lake Van is roughly triangular; 130 kilometres long and fifty kilometres across at the widest stretch. It was created by this volcano, since the lava flow had blocked the basin's river outlet. Now there are no rivers flowing out of the lake, and although many streams feed it the water-level stays fairly constant due to evaporation by the sun. This of course concentrates the level of sodium alkaline in the lake.

Tatvan was an unattractive modern town. The blacksmith didn't have any shoes to fit. People kept crowding me, pulling at Keyif's reins, trying to fiddle with the saddlebags and, when I stopped for tea, the press of people knocked over my glass before I'd even had a sip.

The only amusing moment to lighten my bad mood was when Keyif caught sight of his reflection in a shop's glass window, he charged at it neighing. Then a water-truck came along spraying jets of water out sideways to dampen the dusty streets and Keyif and I got soaked.

I preferred not to ride around the southern rim of the lake since I was eager to reach Van town where Keyif could have a few days' rest, and I knew that ferries have sailed to Van since early history; so I went with Keyif to catch a ferry. His ticket cost the same as mine, 700 Turkish lire (70p), for the four-hour cruise.

Van's era of greatest glory was 2,500 years ago when it became capital of the Urartian empire, but before I could set out to explore its monuments I had to attend to Keyif's needs: a stable for several days with plenty of fodder and new shoes.

The farrier I found was a weather-beaten Kurd of many years' experience, and Keyif stood quietly during the shoeing. The farrier introduced me to a young man who had a spare stable and we negotiated a price which included three daily feeds plus the best clover hay. Then I dumped my luggage at a hotel and late afternoon went out to visit Van Kalesi, a fortress balanced on a lone limestone ridge near the lake shore.

The ridge's cliffs bore great polished rock tabloids of cunei-form inscriptions, whilst along the narrow top the Urartians had built with huge stone blocks, well-squared at the edges, the battlements being added later. A Seljuk influence was discernible through archways edged in small red bricks. Climbing past the citadel, I looked down over the precipice and saw the ruined town of Eski Van (Old Van) lying far below like a street map with floor plans of the buildings' foundations.

It was sunset. Two falcons were hunting, wheeling above the flood plain, and across the lake the volcano Süphan Dağ was silhouetted with orange and grey clouds, lit up and glowing like molten lava.

At the café where I had supper the waiter had some Lake Van cats, white furred, with one green and one brown eye. They are famous in the area, the variant eyes being their trademark. The other special breed of Van cat is the swimming cat, with coffee and white fur. It enjoys swimming and will go chasing the small herrings in the lake, catching them with its claws. But this breed is growing rare and I had to ask around a lot before someone could show me one.

The following day I caught a ferry boat from Gevaş to the island of Aghtamar where the tenth-century King Gagik of Christian Armenia had built his palace and a church which is said to be one of the earliest and finest examples of Romanesque architecture in medieval Christendom; a forerunner of the great Romanesque churches of the Mediterranean.

As the ferry, a small fishing boat, chugged nearer the island I could make out the church, of warm reddish stone in cruciform shape with central dome. My attention was distracted because in the boat some Turkish men were talking about a *bayan* (woman) and her *at* (horse), they must have seen us entering Van.

From the landing stage I hurried up the hill past the overgrown palace gardens and the ruined monastery to the church, and wandered around outside, entranced by the stone relief carvings – lifesize portrayals of David and Goliath, Cain and Abel, Adam and Eve near the tree of knowledge and its serpent, and Daniel with lions licking his feet. To me the most interesting scene was a small one quite high up the south wall. It shows a ship rigged with square sail, and Jonah falling from the ship into a whale's mouth. The whale has scales and a bear's head.

Around the top of the walls is a stone-relief frieze of birds and animals, all flying or running, and above this is a row of human-head gargoyles. Pilgrim graffiti marks the lower exterior, incised crosses of Greek, Latin and Maltese types, some are beautifully intricate with rose-petal or fleur-de-lys shapes. Armenian pilgrims have also scratched prayers and vows on the walls.

Armenian graves are marked by headstones whose floral motifs make a contrast to the abstract geometry of Ahlat's Seljuk graveyard. The sun was blistering hot and the church looked cool inside. As my eyes adjusted to the gloom I saw the interior walls were decorated with a rich profusion of frescoes, telling the story of the New Testament: Joseph's dream with an angel above him; the flight out of Egypt; the massacre of innocents with a long black sword against a faded blue background; Christ raising Lazarus from the dead; riding to Jerusalem on a white donkey; the Last Supper; the Mount of Olives; arrest by Pontius Pilate; the Crucifixion; the angel by the tomb. It was a beautiful picture book drawn on stone.

Around Van over the next few days I found there was no shortage of interesting places to ride, and Keyif was steadily recovering his energy. It only took us ten minutes to reach Toprak Kale, the old palace hill at the back of Van town. The cliffs behind modern Van have Persian inscriptions recording the power of King Xerxes from Persepolis, and at the foot of a mammoth wall is an inscription in Assyrian.

All around Van there are Urartian ruins. What impressed me particularly was the canal and aqueduct system of 1000-600 BC; one canal had stretched sixty kilometres bringing water to twenty-five villages in an otherwise infertile region, with a series of forts to protect it. Forts and castles had been necessary because Van was only 330 kilometres from Nineveh, and these two powerful neighbours were seldom at peace with each other.

Urartian construction utilised the rock's natural shape and topped it with precisely cut and jointed masonry, cyclopean in size. Some building blocks weighed twenty to thirty tons. Inside the walls they built with mud-brick, creating spacious town houses, and temples whose pillars and gabled pediments were forerunners of what later became the classical Greek style. These hilltop complexes were approached by broad curving roads suitable for ox-carts and chariots.

Urartians were good farmers, intelligent builders, and sensible businessmen. Archaeological finds of figurines and portraits on stone and metal depict the Urartians as stocky men with eager expressions; usually in motion, at war, hunting wild beasts, or on horseback. Horse-riding had been a popular sport and King Menua had inscribed on a rock where his horse, Artsibi, had jumped twenty-two cubits (over eleven metres) with the king on his back.

At war this was no barbaric horde, their battledress was similar to the Hittites from whom they probably derived; they wore a broad-belted tunic, and a conical helmet with a flap to protect the back of the neck. One bronze helmet I saw in Van's museum had a row of lions embossed around it, and broad belts were also made of bronze and decorated with horses and lions, hunting and battle scenes. Urartian artistry was so fine that their works were prized in Greece and Italy. Among the booty taken as war trophies from one temple were thirty-three silver chariots, six gold shields and over 350 assorted silver cups.

At the site of Çavustepe I visited a hill fortress of typical massive black masonry, built on the orders of King Sardus in about 750 BC. You can see the bases of wine storage jars one metre in diameter, kept in rows, their shoulders at floor level for stability. Each one could have held 1,000 litres and they were once marked with details of the vintage.

Almost hidden in weeds to one side of a sunken street I found a weighty wine press stone set in a rock vat with a trough carved underneath for the juice to pour down and be collected in jars.

I couldn't resist travelling to Hakkari in the furthest south-east corner where Turkey borders Iraq and Iran. The area is not renowned for tranquillity, though its mountains are rugged and beautiful, for it has long been known as a stronghold of Kurdish unrest.

From Van to Hakkari is 210 kilometres rising in elevation, and on this journey I would be following the route Freya Stark had taken when riding to the Tigris on muleback. I, however, was leaving Keyif to enjoy his rest in his stable and planned to hitch. The way led out along a fertile valley once watered by a Urartu canal, parts of which are still in use. I was given a lift in the back of a truck which I enjoyed for the breeze and glorious open view. I noticed a new reservoir dam being built across the valley's stream, and wondered if it would last as long as the Urartu reservoir just to our north.

Hoşap was my first halt, I climbed out at a fourteenth-century bridge, three-arched with a central plaque; it had been built by a Kurdish ruler, as had the seventeenth-century castle perched on a crag dominating the village.

To reach the castle I had to walk through the police station yard but they didn't mind, and as I climbed the crag I could see that Hoşap had been a large walled town. Long pieces of the wall still stand although the battlements have been eroded into points.

The castle's entrance is through a marvellous round gate-tower with a flight of stone steps leading up into a rock passage of arches that funnel into a courtyard, from which window spaces, decorated with arabesque mouldings and faded paintings of waterlilies, open on three sides high above the village and the valley. The castle had contained hundreds of rooms including two mosques, three bath houses, dungeons, and a tower five storeys high. Now so much has fallen in that only the tops of some doors and windows are visible.

Returning to the village I sat in a small teahouse until I got another truck lift towards Hakkari. The road left the valley and climbed to a pass, then descended to the Zab river which is a tributary of the Tigris. A milky turquoise river, spanned by a couple of suspended footbridges, and an old-fashioned pulley and basket. Until recent years rafts used to ply the river down to Iraq. Now with this new road the rafts are no longer used. The road hugs the gorge and I recalled Dame Freya's description of the rock walls having been polished by centuries of animals rubbing along them to keep away from the vertical drop. Mountains rose steeper and wilder as we approached Hakkari. On a crag beside the town was a ruined castle, now taboo in a military firing zone.

Taking stock in a teahouse I met Salih, a Kurd who had been a mountain guide for ten years, and he offered to show me around the area. So we hitched a lift on a tractor cart going back down to the Zab River. In the gorge we passed an abandoned Nestorian village, and Salih explained that this region had been Nestorian Christian until the end of World War I when they were forced to flee, because they'd made the mistake of siding with the Russians. There were still about a thousand Nestorians living at Beitebab, 200 kilometres to the west.

Salih took me to an old Nestorian church made of irregular stones set in mortar. It had a barrel-vaulted interior with two arches leading from the east apse into a small room with wall niches. Now it was a sheep pen.

We walked up into the hills, wild mint was in mauve flower, and rice was being cultivated on ancient terraces. 'This is one of my friends,' said Salih waving at an old Kurd sitting outside a stone croft. We joined him for an hour and with traditional Kurdish hospitality he brought out some *oltupeynir* (cheese made with herbs) and flat bread. He also gave Salih two live chicks from a wild mountain chicken he'd captured. Salih couldn't give me another name for a mountain chicken and with chicks it's hard to tell but I decided they were probably red-legged partridges which abound here. The birds we call turkeys did not originate in Turkey, and in fact here they're called *hindi* which means India, though actually I thought they originated in the Americas.

The old man seemed contented. He said he had all he required: sheep, fruit trees and rice, spring water, his family and visits from friends. Kurds are not always an aggressive people; I remembered Ardeshir's concern over the dead mouse, and that by tradition Kurds used to defy invasion by retreating with their families and flocks up to higher mountains. Invaders usually only passed through en route to more prosperous lands. Here the Kurds are called Mountain Turks, as a way of dismissing any thoughts of Kurdish nationality. Their language, music and national dress are banned, but they still look different from Turks because by avoiding mixed marriages they have kept their blood and culture Kurdish.

We reached Hakkari by sunset and went to the *çayevi* to drink tea and play backgammon. Local women of course were never permitted to patronise the *çayevi*. An army regiment and band came marching into the main square and stood to attention while playing their national anthem. Everyone in the teashop scrambled to their feet and stood too, even the passersby in the street stopped, and young girls clutching freshly baked bread paused uncertain whether they were allowed to go on home. The military band lacked expertise but made up for it in volume, and the regiment sang lustily, though out of tune. When they finished, everyone's stance unfroze and people carried on with what they had been doing.

Salih was in a huff, his ego was wounded because he had not been served any tea. It was simply that the last teapot was empty and he had to wait for the new one which was slow to boil. Then at the café where we had supper his dish didn't arrive until five minutes after mine so he refused to eat. It was a curious display of male pride and Kurdish ego in a sulk. So we ate in silence. I slept on the sofa of a hotel office and met Salih again in the morning at breakfast time.

His temper had not improved and I went alone down the hill to see the abandoned Nestorian Kilise Medresa, an unremarkable squat building at first glance, until you notice the decorated black and cream stonework of its doorway, carved with arabic script and floral scrolling. Inside is a series of low cells around a courtyard, which suggest it was formerly a monastery, not a church, as its name implies. Each pillar of its cloisters has a different capital: chain design, rope twist, radiating spokes and other geometric patterns.

During Freya Stark's journey one village had given her name to a newly born girl, so somewhere in this region there's a thirty-year-old woman called Freya. Her namesake's route after Hakkari is currently a war zone, and during my visit the area was troubled; there was a flare-up of fighting and a few days later the Turkish air force flew over in hot pursuit of terrorists to drop a couple of bombs. So I caught a bus back to Van and Keyif, and made ready for the next phase of my journey.

16   Bandit border

After Keyif and I had a last bath in Lake Van, we were ready to leave. I collected him from his stable the next morning at 6 a.m., was grossly overcharged but I had expected it, and was content that he'd been well looked after; his girth was one notch fatter.

I was making for Erçek Lake to the north-east, crossing over a mountain divide between the two lakes. At noon I stopped by a stream bank where turquoise kingfishers were diving for their lunch. I rubbed Keyif with some anti-fly treatment I'd bought from a vet, though I doubted it would work since we were too outnumbered; even the vet had been pessimistic but suggested that the flies might feel ill after biting Keyif.

Our afternoon's route lay along a dirt road in a beautiful valley bordered by mountains whose rocky outcrops were pink-red, and at the valley's end I could see a massive natural gateway of vertical rock flanking an empty space of blue sky. To the west it was black and rainy, and the wind was pushing the rain clouds into my valley. There was just about time to outrun the storm, with luck, so I set Keyif into a canter, and felt the first raindrops splatter against my back.

We never quite got caught, always just ahead of the storm. Five storm clouds were converging, and I could see rain falling from all of them, but when I pulled out my plastic rain-sheet Keyif freaked out, rearing up in a panic; it would be impossible for me to wear the rain-sheet and ride, or lead him in it. So much for my rainproofing. Kurdish women in the fields were hastily finishing stacking sheaves of barley; their red clothes making them stand out against the ripe corn.

Passing through the natural rock gateway, Lake Erçek lay below ringed by beaches and cliffs. I turned left up over a headland under an ominously black sky, though there was sun beyond and a rainbow. From the headland a chain of small islands and rocks ran into the lake. We went down for a drink but the water was salty and Keyif spat it out in disgust.

We wandered along the lakeside and over headlands and long beaches. It was evening and people were herding their cattle and horses home. Keyif neighed frantically at them all, he was obviously back in good form.

I spent the night in the lakeshore village of Golalan, at the *muhtar*'s cottage. A kindly man, he told me he had been *muhtar* here for fifteen years, the village didn't bother to hold elections any longer. In various cottages I noticed tapestries and pictures of a legendary creature which the villagers said used to live in the lake. The creature had a man's head with elaborate head-dress on the scaly body of a fish, like a merman except that its tail ended as the head of a serpent. The shape was curled around so that the serpent's forked tongue stuck out toward the man's head. The villagers said the creature's name was Sha Maral, it no longer lives in the lake, nor are there any fish.

We left Erçek Lake on a cart track up the mountains, but I lost the track. The valley led east and I was worried about straying too near the Iranian border. When we passed some cowherds they followed me and kept calling me back. I ignored them since the valley had now swerved north but when I stopped for Keyif to graze, one cowherd caught up and told me that my route would lead into a very bad area. He made throat-slitting gestures to illustrate his meaning.

He took me back to their camp, introduced himself as Ahmet, we drank hot water, since he had no tea, and he invited me on a treasure hunt. Later, at Ahmet's village, I met his brothers. They talked of Urartian gold crowns like the ones I'd seen in the museum at Van and they were convinced I must know something – or else why should I be there? I disappointed them by not having a treasure map to contribute to the enterprise but they decided I'd bring them luck anyway. One of the brothers drew a picture of circles and tree shapes which he said was the key to understanding the site.

I couldn't make head nor tail of their map but was willing to join the adventure. But when it transpired that we would have to go at night, I said no, how could I understand anything in the dark, I'd only trip over rocks. So we agreed to go at dawn. The secrecy was because they thought all the villagers would follow them and take away their prize.

Of the three brothers, Ahmet had the lowest status, no one gave up his cushions to him, or moved up to make room for him. He sat on the plain carpet, and after lunch he cleared away the tray which is usually the work of women. In this village I was treated as a man. I noticed that the women had enormously fat bottoms, wearing numerous wrappings under their skirts, which looked just like bustles. A couple of men here had two wives, one had three, and another had the Moslem maximum of four.

Very early the next morning I went with the brothers to where they thought the Urartian town had been, and they took me to a large rock whose face bore the very ancient inscription which they had drawn on paper for me the day before.

Although much eroded it was easier to understand on the rock than on paper. The circle enclosed a series of ornate crosses, not trees, similar to the Christian pilgrim crosses I had seen on the stonework of Aghtamar's island church in Lake Van. So I explained that I thought the symbols marked a holy grave or tomb.

The brothers had already dug a large hole at the foot of the rock, uncovering the masonry of old walls, and although they dug to shoulder-depth, we found nothing of significance. They decided to abandon that hole, which suited me since I'm not keen on tomb-robbing.

As we parted they gave me a list of villages I should pass through to reach Muradiye, since there was no direct route and they were worried about my safety.

I crossed a forbidding chasm and climbed its opposite side, up into mountains, through the first village on the list and again up a long steep zigzagging climb. From the top I could see both lakes, Lake Erçek behind us and the northern tip of Lake Van ahead.

The track descended and looked as if it were headed down to Lake Van. That didn't suit me so we took off across country along the mountain contour, and by midday had reached an alpine plateau, endlessly rolling and rich with pasture. There were small *yailas*, pink landslides of rock, many fresh springs, streams and turtles. The cool breeze made it a glorious day. We entered a hidden plain extending about ten kilometres, Keyif cantered along in top form, he simply wasn't interested in walking, and his excitement added to my sense of exhilaration. It was a memorably wonderful ride.

I stopped four times to let Keyif eat, roll and relax, and mid-afternoon we paused at a hamlet so I could have lunch, but rather regretted it because of silly young men and no stable for Keyif who got left in the sun and wouldn't touch the thistle-full hay that the villagers gave him. The silliness of the youths was mostly because they too were convinced I'd got a treasure map – it's odd how people were obsessed with treasure hunting, and they wanted me to give them my gun, which I don't have, and didn't I know any karate or self-defence, which made me think they were planning to rob me. Also I had a tick inside my trouser leg which I couldn't get at to kill.

So I left after half an hour, keeping a sharp watch-out behind me for followers, and we sped over the hills. Still going north, down through a boulder field and sloping mountain spur; gently down, the major descent would come later. I hadn't realised how high we had gone.

A movement attracted my eyes, the lumbering of a brown bear, fortunately moving away from us. I was told that they could be quarrelsome when coming out of hibernation. Later I spotted another hamlet and thought there should be a way down from it but the track proved to be an animal path which clung to the side of a ravine. At times I felt sure I had mislaid the right way and was only on a goat path. This was probably true, since by halfway down the slopes became perilous, and the path narrowed along a sheer drop. I slipped dislodging some stones that fell vertically for fifteen metres. The inner side of the path had such prickly thistles that leaning inwards was impossible. In patches the path had eroded away leaving gaps that Keyif stepped over gingerly.

At one steep patch I slid down on my back, holding the reins to stop my fall. Keyif stood firm. Very testing for him, the worst I had asked of him so far, but he wasn't fazed by it. The steepness of the angles necessitated a crupper to stop my saddle and saddlebags sliding forward on to the horse's neck, and I suddenly realised that the tasselled woven strap which hung from the back of the saddle was not only decorative. I fitted it as a crupper and it worked well.

Crossing landslides and loose scree, I tended to go down toboggan-wise and wished that Keyif wouldn't keep taking a higher route. If he slipped I would be cushioning his fall!

The descent took three hours, and we came down into a valley beyond the north-east tip of Lake Van. I stopped at a village for tea, and let them persuade me to stay the night. The men here also asked me about treasure maps, and showed me some local rock-inscriptions of crosses, square W's and other squiggles. We had rice pudding running with butter for supper. The night was one of heat, mosquitoes, and bed bugs that put red weals on my stomach and legs.

In the morning as I rode out of the village, a dog the size of a Saint Bernard bounded up to attack. I drew up my knees and rattled Keyif's reins as if to tell him 'Do something', and when the dog tried to bite Keyif's hind legs, the horse kicked back. But one got me later that day as I was walking along the road to Çaldiran. A large Anatolian came bounding out of a shed snarling furiously. I did the worst possible thing, I ran, and felt its teeth snap into my leg. Pain and fear shot through me but luckily the dog let go and ran back into the shed. I limped away, wondering if not having a tetanus injection would be more harmful than a visit to the local hospital, if there was one.

I decided to look for anti-tetanus vaccine in Çaldiran, the next town, which we reached at sunset. Someone yelled '*Turist, gel, gel*' (come here) so I went to ask where to find a water tap for the horse, and I stayed there, with Keyif in the empty cottage next door. My host killed a chicken for supper which we ate with melon and watermelon. It was a cold evening, I put on a sweater and at night was grateful for the thick quilt.

The hospital was not open at 8 a.m. so I went to the nurses' house. The nurses were delightful, though the dispensary was waiting for a new supply of anti-tetanus vaccine, due to arrive some day soon, but the girls assured me that the hospital at Doğubayazit should have some. And they gave me a little bag of sweets for the journey as a touching gesture of goodwill.

I rode north across a great flat plain where the battle of Çaldiran had been fought in 1514, when the Ottoman Sultan Selim the Grim had decisively defeated the Persian army before forging on to conquer Syria and Palestine.

Our road led close to the Iranian border. A dirt road with parts still under construction, in a year's time it would be asphalted, but now it was perfect for a horse.

Lonely and desolate, we pattered through a vastness where black rock was eroded in turbulent seas of jagged teeth. A strong wind kept the day cool and emphasised the desolation. I paid attention to the slightest movement, being aware that there was a very real danger of bandits.

As the land unfolded I saw a distant crater of a large volcano to the west and realised that the jagged expanses of black rock were actually huge tongues of lava. The volcano's cone was topped with snow, and the patches between the black tongues were verdant green, a startling combination. Keyif danced along, giving me a top-quality ride.

We reached an army outpost, here to guard the frontier, and

the sentry called me over to check my passport. He looked at
the photograph, then at me, and queried '*Bayan*?' (woman?).
Other soldiers came over and seemed equally puzzled so I took
off my man's cap and let my long blonde hair show. This earned
me an invitation into the office for a glass of tea under the
regulation portrait of Atatürk. The soldiers were patriotic young
men doing their eighteen months' national service on one of
the remotest frontiers. They had no transport to go into town,
their supplies being brought in by truck, so they never left their
station except to make foot patrols in the mountains. They
claimed they didn't mind the discipline and it occurred to me
this was just as well. Without discipline, they might all have
leapt on me like a roomful of Keyifs with one mare.

The soldiers said that martial law had ended this week in
eastern Turkey. I hadn't known the region was in that state.
They also said there would be three more military outposts
along the road, and warned me that when I descended into the
lowlands I would pass through a notoriously wild and lawless
place called Kizil Ka where even they dare not stop, and their
vehicles have frequently been stoned. Those people are the
worst type of Kurd they told me, lawless and violent bandits.
The commander added that there was no alternative route, I
would have to ride through Kizil Ka, but I should keep my wits
sharp.

At the second military outpost the soldiers were playing
volleyball. My passport was checked and the news relayed that
here was a girl, and when I explained that I'd ridden from
Erzurum via Van they all began to applaud.

Later, passing through a windswept empty area, I looked
for a hidden niche where Keyif and I could take an hour's
undisturbed rest. The giant lava flow with its grassy inlets
offered concealment, and some way back from the road I found
a good space, unloaded the baggage, tethered Keyif and, suddenly, realised that we were not alone. Someone else was
hiding here too. I could see his feet in worn leather boots
sticking out from behind some rocks and, thank goodness, he
was asleep.

My first instinct was to flee, but not without my horse and
baggage. At that moment Keyif found the stranger and snorted,
waking him. The man was startled, he scuttled backwards and
hissed at Keyif. Then cautiously he poked his head out from
behind the rocks. My heart was pounding, but it occurred to

me that perhaps the man was just as frightened as I was. We stared at each other for a frozen moment. His was the unkempt face of a thin twenty-year-old who had not shaved for weeks. His expression was very wary. I couldn't think how to react, so in the end I waved my hand at him politely and greeted him in Turkish. His head poked out further and he replied not in Turkish, but Farsi.

He walked over and scrutinised me then asked 'Do you speak English?' I nodded, my surprise left me speechless. He asked for food, saying he'd hardly eaten for a week, so I gave him my picnic lunch of bread, eggs and tomato. I meant for us to share the picnic but he ate so ravenously I let him finish it. Between mouthfuls he talked and I pieced together his story.

A fugitive, deserting from the Iranian army, he had walked for eight days through the Kurdistan mountains to seek asylum in Turkey. He had been afraid to walk by day because the Iranian army or Revolutionary Guards would have shot at him, mistaking him for a Kurd; and afraid to walk on moonlit nights because the Kurds would have shot him, mistaking him for a Revolutionary Guard.

He was well-educated and spoke English fluently, and explained his reason for deserting. 'I was likely to die crossing those mountains, but I was sure to die if I stayed in Khomeni's army.'

He bombarded me with questions, did I know where there was a collection point for other Iranian deserters? Actually yes, I did know because in Van I had met a group of them most of whom had paid the Kurdish mountain-folk about $1500 each to bring them out on horseback. Even their stories had been gruelling, riding by night in constant danger. So I told him the name of the place where he could find the others, and explained that as I understood it from them, UNESCO gives $500 for each man's food and lodging, but that he was not yet safe since Iran offers $1000 for every man sent back. After twenty days in Turkey he could apply for work, and would need to go to Istanbul to ask UNESCO for a passport. But it would not be easy and his Iranian money was almost worthless here in Turkey.

As Keyif and I approached the third military post I heard some shots from up ahead. Creeping forward and scanning the mountains, I noticed the movement of a man on a hill summit attracting the attention of a second man on another summit. It seemed reasonable to suppose they were soldiers on lookout duty. They didn't appear agitated, probably they were just firing to make sure their rifles worked.

There was no trouble and I cleared the checkpost without delay. They said it was twenty-five kilometres to Doğubayazit, the same distance as both other checkposts had told me! Beyond it the mountains became beautiful with thick meadow grasses and the black tents of nomadic *yailas* dotted across the undulating vastness. This was one of the most scenically glorious roads I had used so far.

We had not yet reached the notorious Kizil Ka; Kizil means red, so I stayed alert for some sign. The land to the west fell away in a series of parallel mountain ridges outlined against each other. Suddenly we came over a hilltop into a magnificent panorama with snow-covered Mount Ararat looming above the mountainous horizon.

Mount Ararat is unequalled in the world for the height it rises above its surroundings. Even Mount Everest at nearly 10,000 metres is only about 3,500 metres above the glaciers which define its base. Ararat's summit is 4,270 metres above the plain of Doğubayazit, although in total altitude the mountain is only 5,180 metres. Its height is made more impressive by its shape and solitary position, growing from a flat plain almost without foothills. Ararat was still far away yet already it seemed to fill the sky.

Closer to me, about one kilometre ahead, was a massive pyramidal triangle of red rock. This was the red sign I had been watching for. The village shortly after it would be Kizil Ka. I dismounted to collect a pocketful of stones (for retaliation), and decided to try going through the village on foot, which might look less aggressive. Though the dogs could be a problem, and I left my stirrups ready for quick mounting.

It was a fairly successful idea, but I could tell that Keyif was being peppered by small stones because he pranced along fast. I smiled and greeted the elder villagers, it was only the urchins and youths who threw stones. Once clear of the village I swung into the saddle and we galloped away. Stones rattled behind us but we were quickly out of range. However I was congratulating myself too soon.

A man on horseback galloped up behind us and, instead of passing, he slowed to keep pace with Keyif. This was potentially a bad sign. So I made polite conversation with him; admired his horse, told him about my journey, and my husband in the next town. Keyif was snorting and I warned the man that he would kick and strike if the other horse came too close. Keyif played the part well. At one point the man tried to make Keyif throw me, but I'd kept Keyif's mouth so soft that he was easy to bring under control.

When we reached a flock of sheep and three shepherd youths, the horseman said goodbye. I was relieved. But the shepherds blocked my path waving sticks and demanding money. I politely asked the horseman to tell them to let me through. He did try to help me, and chased off one of the shepherds but the others attacked me with sticks and stones. The road was so steep and rocky it was impossible to run, and the road sides were even rockier. Pure violence was written on the shepherds' faces. They knew they had me cornered. Keyif reared and plunged as the shepherds brandished their sticks and pelted us with hefty sized rocks. One hit my shoulder and another just missed my head.

We weren't going to get past without help so I commanded my ally on horseback to come over. He came and Keyif dodged behind his horse, passing the shepherds who then leapt at my saddlebags, tearing into them with their hands, but Keyif danced clear before they had managed to break anything. I remembered the stones in my pockets and began to hurl them at the youths. Their eyes went murderous, and they ran at me.

Clapping my heels to Keyif's sides we didn't quite manage to get away before they had grabbed the back pocket of one saddlebag and my reins. I kicked one youth in the ribs to make him let go, and Keyif responded to my gallop command. The youth at the back clung on for several paces before letting go. Keyif and I raced down the steep track.

Several times Keyif nearly fell, but the hail of rocks still hitting him and me deterred him from slowing down. We had escaped. Glancing at my saddlebags I saw that the shepherds had succeeded in stealing my water-flask, Keyif's tether, and a few other things. But we weren't going back.

It was sunset, I stopped at the next village and asked if there was a safe place where Keyif and I could stay the night, explaining that I'd just had a bad experience in Kizil Ka. The men were stroppy, looking at me with unfriendly eyes, no one would take the responsibility of housing me. They suggested I kept on riding.

'Nothing would make me ride in this hostile place at night,' I retorted. 'My horse is tired, we need shelter.'

A boy was ordered to take me to a military camp beside the village, where I dismounted and shook hands with the apparently senior men before voicing my request. Not that I wanted to stay at their camp, just to make sure they would treat me with respect. The *muhtar* happened to be there and he said that I would be welcome to stay at his house, and my horse would be safe in his stable because his property was enclosed behind walls whose outer gate was locked at night.

During the evening he told me that he had been the *muhtar* for five years and he certainly didn't want to be elected for another term, the work was all forms of trouble. He and his family were delightful people, I wished I wasn't too worn out to enjoy the evening. The night was abysmal, the bedding full of fleas, I awoke every few minutes and eventually just sat waiting for morning to come. It seemed likely to me that it's only the bedding which is stored without regular use that has fleas. Extra quantities of bedding are a status symbol, but it can go unused for years. At breakfast the *muhtar* asked me if I had slept well, I didn't have the heart to tell him the truth.

Rather than take the road to Doğubayazit and Mount Ararat, still twenty-five kilometres away around a mountain barrier, I decided to try a short cut over the mountains. The *muhtar* agreed that one of the ravines would take me the right way. After passing the fourth military checkpoint I turned east, it was easy to keep my bearings since Mount Ararat towered into the sky way above the nearer mountain horizon. At the end of the plain we began climbing into hills, using a dry riverbed. It steepened into a ravine, progress was possible on a sheep path, but it changed course and as we closed in under the mountains I lost sight of Ararat's peak. So we went by God and by guesswork. My saddlebags got torn by rocks along the inside of a narrow cliff ledge but I stuffed a plastic bag under the tear and it plugged the gap.

At the head of the ravine was a spring, Keyif and I both tried to drink from it but he muddied the pool. Above this was a hill crest, we hurried up it, I was impatient to see whether I had picked the right ravine. We went over the crest, but another bigger crest lay ahead. Then slowly I saw the summit of Ararat appearing above my ridge, growing taller with every few metres that I climbed. Cloudless snowy flanks, smooth sweeping cone stretching down towards earth level, it seemed to keep growing until I reached the crest and then it lay before me, straight ahead.

From my highland vantage point I could also see the town of Doğubayazit still a few hours away down on the plain, and the ancient palace of Isak Paşa, which I hoped to visit later.

Near me on a mountain shoulder a Kurdish shepherd was brewing tea. He called me over; for obvious reasons I wasn't feeling friendly toward Kurdish shepherds but my desire for a cup of tea overcame my reluctance. He had two hundred sheep and he showed me how he played his flute to them. Its notes were reedy and zingy and its song carried on the breeze among the sheep and over the hills. My faith in human nature began to flow back into me.

He also showed me his favourite sheep, a woolly ram whose corkscrew horns indicated his descent from wild moufflons. Some young shepherd boys sauntered over to say hello, and respectfully called me Agha, a man's title. I thought about the line between distrust and caution, and how I prefer to trust people than to expect the worst, believing that in general one has a choice over whether one brings out the good or the bad in people.

Time stood still, it was a scene which didn't seem to have changed since men wrote about shepherds in the Bible.

Filling the background was the mighty Ararat, a mountain revered as holy by Christians, Moslems and Jews. On impulse I asked the old man if he thought that Noah's Ark was on Mount Ararat, and his reply was an unhesitating yes. He said all the local people know it's there, though they haven't seen it.

17 Noah was here

The descent to the town was long but not difficult, we reached it at noon and I put Keyif in a public stable run by a half-wit.

My first chore was to go to the hospital and have an anti-tetanus injection against the dogbite. My leg didn't hurt any longer, in fact the skin had gone numb which was worrying but the bite was healing well. After the injection I stopped at a chemist for flea powder, then went to the army headquarters. My purpose here was to try and obtain a new water-flask from their stores, to replace the stolen one, since it was impossible to buy a proper metal flask in the town shops, and the cheap plastic bottles on offer would split with rough handling.

In explaining why I needed a replacement flask the soldiers misunderstood what I wanted and they took me to the gendarmerie who promised to try and get back my original flask. It seemed they were longing for an excuse to teach Kizil Ka a lesson. That was fine by me and I hoped they would succeed. They told me to report back the next morning.

As I walked down the road two young school-girls latched on to my hands. Laughing and skipping, they led me to their home and invited me to stay. They were learning English at school, so I gave them an hour's reading practice in the afternoon.

Later I walked out of town to visit Isak Paşa. The palace is visible from afar, perched in a dominating position among sharp escarpments of green rock; its walls, dome and minaret stood out in sunlight against a black, threatening sky. Built in the 1700s by a Kurdish chieftain, its style is a mixture of Seljuk, Ottoman, Georgian, Armenian and Iranian. The entrance is magnificent, even without the gold-plated doors which the Russians took away during their 1917 invasion. Inside the first courtyard ornate stonework is carved in the Iranian style of animals and flowers instead of Moslem geometric motifs. Beneath the mosque a marble staircase leads to the graves of

Isak Paşa and one of his wives. There is a warren of small interconnecting rooms and dead ends and since I was being followed by a young man I climbed on to the walls, and toured the palace from above.

The floor of the throne room is superbly tiled in black and white marble and it has carved stone pillars, while each small individual room of the harem and children's apartments has its own fireplace with an elegant half-conical mantel, chimney breast and windows. The sky behind the palace now glowed as late sun lit the black clouds.

Isak Paşa seemed deserted except for its caretaker and my Kurdish shadow. He came up to me as I left and said he was also walking back to Doğubayazit. Rain began falling, increasing in ferocity until hailstones were stingingly painful. We sheltered in a ruined building and although the man was most helpful about pointing out the various other ruins in the jumble of fallen masonry covering the mountainside, he was very tedious with his suggestions of how we could keep warm together. I said that if I didn't hurry back to Doğubayazit my large jealous husband would be angry; and despite the rain I opted to run down the mountain, taking off my sandals and using a short cut to meet the road at the bottom. The man ran with me, to show me the way, quite amicably still offering me his body every time I paused for breath. Apart from that the views were stunning and the short turf with its stubby red flowers and feathery plants underfoot made for lovely running.

The man finally gave up on me and soon afterwards I reached the road. Still three kilometres to go, and still pouring cold rain, so when a tractor and cart came along I accepted a lift. The four young men in the cab offered to let me drive and since the driver's seat was safer than being squashed in their midst, I drove. I hadn't driven a tractor before, the cart made it swing around and slow to accelerate, but with four men trying to grope me I put my foot flat on the pedal and hoped the load of sheep in the trailer wouldn't fall out.

The roadsides banked steeply and I couldn't see the potholes because the windshield was caked in mud. More mud came flying up from the wheels into the cab, but without mishap we reached the school-girls' house and I jumped out. They were just sitting down to supper, tablecloth on floor, the girls tucked the cloth into their shirt necks. What a sensible idea. And we all dipped into the communal bowls of meat stew, pasta, yoghurt, and salad, a delicious meal. Despite the humble appearance of the house, the family was obviously not poor. They had a television, video, fridge, and a servant girl who was an orphaned relative. Listening to the news on television I heard that there had been an earthquake a few nights previously in this region. Although I must have slept through it, the shock waves had stretched to Ankara.

In the morning when I went to feed Keyif I found that chickens had nested overnight in his manger. They hadn't allowed Keyif to eat his hay, and they had laid two eggs in it. I moved him into a private room, fed him and shut the door so the chickens could not tease him any more.

As arranged, I reported to the gendarmerie and was surprised and impressed to see my water flask and horse ropes lying on the desk. I congratulated the men on their efficiency. The rest of the day was spent quietly writing letters and mending the tears in my saddlebags, until 6 p.m. when I went to give Keyif his evening feed. The stables were locked and the half-wit had gone home. I couldn't leave it at that because I wanted Keyif to gain weight, he needed to eat plenty, so I started looking for a way in.

The local children who had accompanied me to the stables said they could get in through the roof. We climbed on to the flat roof and found a series of small ventilation holes. I knew that one of them had a shallow drop to an empty loft beside Keyif's stall, and I managed to squeeze through it. The drop was head height, but it wasn't until I climbed down into Keyif's stall that I remembered that I had bolted his door against the chickens. His hay and barley were in the next room. So I tried to climb out, and couldn't make it. I got my arms out but could get no leverage to lift myself. Hopelessly stuck, the situation was so absurd that I began to laugh. It's silly what people assume they can do. Finally a boy climbed down and let me stand on his back to get out.

Then we did what I should have done in the first place, went to the house of the stable-keeper, and he unlocked the stables for me. In the meantime another horse had arrived to be stabled overnight. I brought Keyif out for water, he took one sniff at the other horse, a mare, and lunged at her.

I couldn't hold him and my feet slid through the wet dung on the floor. The mare was kicking at Keyif, I was pulling with all my might, the mare's owner was shouting, I got kicked by the mare and trodden on by Keyif as he leapt on to her back, trying to rape her. Fortunately he missed and I managed to wrap his tether around a pole and pulled him away.

The man quickly took his mare into another stall and I apologised, leading Keyif away in disgrace. Life was never dull.

Mount Ararat, I pondered which way to ride up it. We must assume that Noah was the first man to climb down Ararat. But the first to climb up it was a German called Dr Parrot who made the ascent in 1829. The easy approach from Doğubayazit didn't appeal to me since today most climbing groups go that way and it sounded crowded. When you've got a whole mountain, why follow the beaten track?

A south-east route would have taken me up on to the col between the great and small Ararats, but this alpine pastureland would be full of Kurdish *yailas*, and I had been told stories of a couple of American climbers who had everything stolen, including their boots.

The north and east faces of Ararat look into Russia and the area is prohibited to tourists, a shame because from there one can see up the abyss, a 3,000-metre chasm that splits the mountainside up to its summit massif, and it is overhung by 1,000 metres of glaciers. So Keyif and I would try a western approach. Once there was a village called Ahora and a monastery dedicated to St James on the north side of the mountain but both were destroyed by the massive earthquake of 1840 which threw the Araxes river out of its bed in the plain below. Today a new village stands nearby, and the north side has the added curiosity of a rocky outcrop shaped like the prow of a ship, which has often been mistaken for the Ark.

I liked the idea of looking for Noah's Ark. Soon after the 1840 earthquake there had been various sightings of the Ark, the first by a team of Turkish surveyors and workmen who went to check for danger of avalanches. They reported finding the front section of a large boat protruding from a glacier. Experts were sent to examine it and they climbed into some of the boat's well-preserved storage holds, but complete examination was not possible since most of it was still enclosed in ice.

In 1893 the highly respected Archdeacon of Babylon and Jerusalem, Dr Nouri, launched an expedition. He too found the Ark and announced that he had entered the bows and stern, although the central part was still icebound. He mentioned very thick hull timbers held together by 300-centimetre pegs. The archdeacon was an intelligent and educated man, speaking over ten languages, and a friend of the American President Roosevelt, and it seemed unlikely that his story was a hoax.

Other reports came from Russian pilots during the First World War; stories that were initially laughed at then checked out by senior officers, who agreed it was true, the Ark was still there. The Tsar authorised an army expedition. It returned with photographs, but these were lost during the Russian Revolution.

In the Second World War another Russian expedition claimed to have located the Ark, badly rotted by this time and in the process of submerging back into a glacier.

While I was riding through Turkey, an American had been applying for permission to dig for Noah's Ark. He believed he knew where it now lay and was coming armed with special electronic equipment. But at the last minute the Turkish authorities had rescinded his permit and decided to investigate his spot for themselves. I felt a little sorry for him. Personally I didn't expect to find the Ark, but that didn't stop me from looking.

The next morning dawned clear, and Keyif and I set out via the corn-merchant, where I strapped some extra barley in a sack behind the saddle, and saluted the gendarmes who had recovered my stolen goods. It took only ten minutes to leave town, Keyif was so fresh he raced along skittishly and shied at every vehicle on the road.

Once clear of the town we headed towards the west side of the mountain, aiming to run up between two parallel arms of lava. Before long the land underfoot became spongy and I could see reedbeds and marshland ahead so we detoured to the west and tried again. The morning sun was building up a hellish heat, yet high above were glaciers.

The slopes were extremely tricky, the giant lava flows were jagged with crevasses that Keyif could not cross, the land between lava tongues was boggy, much wetter than would be expected after rainfall, and it made me agree with the recent scientific theory that Mount Ararat contains a vast lake inside its bulk. People had warned me that water is a curious problem on Ararat because although there is a massive ice-cap there are very few springs or streams. And their length is short, they flow back into holes in the mountainside. A vast subterranean cavern is plausible when one considers the inner working of molten volcanic activity, and it ties in with the last eruption producing steam and gases instead of lava.

Reaching an area where the marsh had dried to a crazy-paving of crusty slabs I heaved a sigh of relief. Keyif was less sure, he didn't like the fissures between them and he was not at all keen to walk where I directed him. At first the crust supported his weight and we progressed quite far until suddenly it gave way.

The slabs cracked and dust exploded upwards. Keyif floundered, thrashing with his legs but was unable to find any firm foothold, and we were sinking fast. I was almost blinded with dust and shock; realising the dry bog was probably made of volcanic ash, possibly bottomless.

We had already sunk down over one metre, but Keyif had managed instinctively to turn around and was plunging desperately towards the point where we had entered. All I could do was cling on to his mane and shout encouragement.

That was the first of many dry and wet quagmires that we fell into over the next twenty-four hours while Mount Ararat lived up to its popular reputation as a mountain that does not wish to be climbed. Ancient nomads believed it was guarded by angels and forbidden to men. A lot of talk nowadays centres on its dangers, like the zone of snakes. But I would see for myself.

Keyif and I were battling into a strong headwind and I could feel rain drops coming from behind us. With luck the wind would push the rain away. We reached about 3,000 metres; I wondered how long it would be before Keyif began feeling the effects of the altitude.

This western side, even down on the plain, is almost uninhabited and uncultivated, there seems to be no water. Above us tall rocks reached up like spires. The eastern plain is more populated, with villages that bear names such as Nakhitchevan, meaning 'the place where Noah disembarked', and there is a site called Noah's burial place, and Ahora which means 'vine plantation'. Among the birds and beasts saved by the Ark, Noah also brought a collection of plants, and the vine was one of them.

The book of Genesis (chapter 9, verse 20) tells that Noah planted a vine after landing on Ararat. His son, Shem, took vines with him to the south-east and south-west. In fact, this geographical region is said to be the original home of the vine and, as I'd seen near Lake Van, it was an early centre for vine cultivation with sophisticated techniques of wine-making by 800 BC.

Despite the headwind, rain was now lashing down. As before, Keyif panicked at the crackle of my rainproof sheet and I had to fold it away. There was no point in seeking shelter since we were already soaked. I had noticed some *yailas*, but Keyif had spotted their horses and he began stamping and whinnying. That mare in Doğubayazit had scrambled his brains. Even the faintest horse-like shape in the distance made him prance with excitement.

The rain eased to drizzle and finally to wet mist. When I opened my saddlebags to put on dry clothes I discovered that rain had funnelled in through a hole in the plastic lining and everything was damp. The two most vital items were my sleeping bag, now useless, and my notebook, also useless because a biro doesn't write on wet paper. A pencil would have worked but I didn't have one. Weighing up my feelings about a cold wet bed against my mistrust of the Kurds here, I stopped overnight at a *yaila*. The women helped me to dry out my clothes on their dung-fuelled fire, and were as kind and hospitable as Kurds can be. Keyif was a bundle of energy, racing to and fro on his tether and roaring at the mares, he had no interest in food, water or sleep.

Dawn was misty, and when I went to collect Keyif he seemed to have no outline, just a grey blur in a grey fog. He was still prancing with energy, his mane streaming out and his nostrils steaming. A cold damp morning, I shivered uncomfortably and we got rather lost because mist shrouded the whole landscape; billowing and thinning, putting stark lines into soft focus. At our highest point I saw, looming blackly out of the opalescent blur, the tall prow-like shape of the Ark Rock. From this angle it certainly did look convincingly like a ship.

A shepherd I met said that the mist could stay for days. That was enough for me and I headed Keyif downhill. As we came down we reached the level where the clouds ended and beneath us was warm sunshine. Below that, the descent through lava spews grew continually hotter until around us was a volcanic bomb-field, scorching under a relentless sun.

I didn't mind about not reaching the summit. One cannot fail unless one sets out to succeed. Goals are like destinations, they don't always matter. Our journey was enough in itself.

18 A consumer's guide to Kurdish farriers

I was now on my way to Digor over a sub-tropical plain growing cotton, pomegranates, vines and olives. We stayed overnight in Iğdir and next day were forced on to a stretch of asphalt which I hated. From the sound of Keyif's hooves I could tell that he had a loose shoe. So much for the Van farrier who said these shoes would last for two months, they were worn out after two weeks.

At noon we rested in a shady patch of lucerne, I bought a loaf of bread off a passing donkey-cart and a man gave me some tomatoes to go with it. Rather more tomatoes than I could eat, he was adamant that I must put the extras in my saddlebags, so I did but was sure they would squish all over my luggage.

The Russian frontier was only two kilometres away and I could see a border fence and a watchtower. The canal I tried to follow in the afternoon went too close to the border. Suddenly whistles were blown and, knowing that tourists have been shot by Russian guards for going too close to the border, I wasted no time in turning around and heading inland.

It was a grilling hot day; hot wind, sand bare but for stones and thorn plants. The frontier ran parallel with our course, it looked oppressive with frequent watchtowers, their metal legs and silvery tops made me think of Martian invasions. They linked a high wire fence, and beyond it I could see a small Russian village. On the Turkish side a conical volcano sat ahead.

Late afternoon we reached a canyon and river, then the village of Tuzluca where I asked for the blacksmith. He was a young man and clearly afraid of Keyif's back feet. Although Keyif stood long enough for the farrier to remove his hind shoes, he wouldn't let the man put the new shoes on.

Patience would have worked, but the young farrier was so nervous he jumped away whenever Keyif moved. Someone put stones in Keyif's ears and twisted them, and instead of

calming the horse it upset him. Then the farrier complained
that he had scratched his finger, so I retorted, 'You're supposed
to know what you're doing.' Admittedly Keyif had by this time
grown wild and impossible. The farrier lost his temper and he
hit Keyif on the nose with his hammer, so I yelled at the man.
He was upset, Keyif was upset, it was pointless trying to finish
the shoeing that evening, so we agreed to meet again in the
morning, though I had my doubts since it is easier to shoe a
tired horse than a fresh one.

That exasperating farrier never reappeared in the morning,
but another was found. I hadn't realised there was a choice.
Not that this one was any better. He tried to put ropes round
Keyif's hind legs but Keyif kicked them away. So he tied Keyif's
nose and mouth shut with a tight rope. His theory was sound,
for he was imitating a twitch, which is a common way of
tranquillising a horse. It squeezes a nerve in the end of the
nose, without causing pain, more like an anaesthetic.

But none of the men knew how to tie a twitch and they tied
poor Keyif's nose in knots. He still wouldn't let them near his
feet. They decided to make him tired, the farrier took him for
a gallop, I kept saying my horse would only get excited not
tired, it would take fifty kilometres to quieten him enough for
shoeing. The infuriating thing was that no one would listen to
me because I'm a woman. It wouldn't have mattered if the
farrier hadn't un-shod two of Keyif's feet the previous day.
There was no point in waiting while they all galloped about on
Keyif, so I put my saddlebags on his back and left.

Keyif and I used an abandoned road, its bridges had long
been washed away but we found ways down and up. My frayed
temper began to cool. The land opened up, with a low volcanic
cone to my left and many vibrantly coloured earthen hills,
layered with dramatic red and green bands, rain-eroded and
soft. To our right the Araxes River marked the Russian border.
This valley has long been important for its fertile soil and the
unusual concentration of minerals – copper, gold, silver, iron,
aluminium, lead, zinc, mercury, arsenic and borax. It was
known for copper and bronze-work from 3000 BC, the craftsmen
producing fourteen different types of alloys.

We came to a red earth road and turned right along it, heading
for Digor about forty kilometres away. Watchtowers sprouted
from the hills on both sides of the frontier. The villagers said
there was absolutely no communication across the border, and

even when they saw people on the opposite side of the river-bank, they never spoke to them.

We climbed an escarpment and entered a long arid plateau. The only person I saw that afternoon was a man who tried to attack me, but he was easily dissuaded and I escaped on Keyif. As the sun began setting I grew worried that we might have to camp overnight which would be very uncomfortable without a windbreak or water, so I urged Keyif faster despite his unshod feet. The barrenness had to end somewhere.

At 8 p.m. we reached an area of scant cultivation, but no water. Then I noticed a movement and picked out the figures of some men only two kilometres away. The twilight flashed on their long scythes, as they went home from the fields. When they heard Keyif's pounding hooves, their surprise was total but they understood my predicament and offered to take me to their village, an hour distant in a ravine and hidden from sight.

They were Kurds, and their wives were away at a *yaila*, but they were respectful, treating me as a man, and I enjoyed their company. They took me to see a square-hewn baptismal font which they'd brought from a ruined church on the border. It had three angels carved on one side, and the men had lovingly patched the stone where it had been broken. At night we could see across to some Russian villages, lit by electricity. We had oil-lamps; I was told that a powerline would arrive here next year. But Turkish villages have other facilities and, travelling with Keyif, I really appreciated Atatürk's legacy of stone drinking-fountains bringing spring water to villages, with lower troughs for livestock.

It was a full morning's ride to Digor, we kept up a fast pace cantering much of the way. I was hoping to tire Keyif so he wouldn't resist a blacksmith. However, in Digor, the only one I could find was unable to work because his tools were at his home village, Alem, fifteen kilometres to the north. So I arranged to meet him there next day.

Meanwhile I was offered a stable and a bed by a family of lace-makers. Their living room was small and innumerable daughters sat plying their crochet needles busily. The lace was exquisite, and the girls chattered without needing to look at their work. When I asked about ancient ruins in the area they told me that four kilometres up the valley was a place called Beş Kilise (Five Churches).

I rode there when the afternoon sun cooled, mislaying the

path several times because I couldn't really believe it went up the side of the gorge. A man came running up from behind and I recognised him as Yilmaz, an uncle of the lace-making girls. He was puffed for breath, he had run all the way from Digor since he knew I would never find the path without guidance. He stopped for a moment's breather and I noticed he was sitting on an old fallen stone cross, its face inscribed with scrolled patterns.

The path took us below tall cliffs yet above the chasm of the gorge. Yilmaz told me the river is called Karsçai and its water is reputed to be good for rheumatism, stomach and heart complaints. The five churches had stood on the edge of the gorge, where the rock falls vertically down over a hundred metres. Four are so ruined they are almost indiscernible but for their red stone masonry mottled with grey lichen. The fifth church is standing, its dome still perfectly intact but its octagonal walls have deep cracks. Yilmaz said the church was 'saat guneş', a sundial! The monks would have told the time by the sunlight's angle through the eight open arches. It was ingenious.

We lingered there until sundown, Yilmaz kept saying there was no hurry because he knew his way in the dark, he had roamed here since childhood. The first time he came here was aged six, on a picnic with his father and eighteen brothers and sisters. However I insisted that we got moving since I wanted to try a different way back along the bottom of the gorge.

We picked our way down to the foot of the pinkish-red cliffs, pock-marked with erosion. The river was strewn with boulders, not easy to ride across but we had to cross and recross at almost every bend. Big crabs scuttled out of our way, and above us in the cliffs I glimpsed some three-storey caves which Yilmaz said were inhabited long before the Byzantine era.

Yilmaz kept suggesting we stop while my horse grazed; I was hoping he had no ulterior motives. It was boring always having to be aware of this potential threat as a routine part of daily life. He did proposition me, but accepted my refusal with good humour.

Arriving back at Digor I was informed that the Commandant of Gendarmes wanted to see my passport immediately. The Commandant was about to sit down to a rather sumptuous dinner which he invited me to join. He was beautifully mannered, though somehow he kept knocking things over; glasses, bottles, and the table.

When he asked where I was going I explained about the farrier at Alem. The Commandant said that was fine and suggested I should continue along that track to reach the fabled site of Ani where there had once been a city of 1,001 churches.

This sounded a good idea and next morning I saddled Keyif and set out for Alem. I was obviously the first tourist to visit Alem since most of the villagers ran behind me and when the farrier took me into his cottage everyone crowded in too, those who couldn't fit inside peering through the window, a sea of faces in colourful headshawls of red and yellow. One lady who pushed her way into the middle of the room was standing bewildered looking for the reason for this mob. She glanced past me several times before she spotted the difference and then her face broke into an enormous grin.

The imam came in and everyone struggled to their feet in respect. He talked in a booming voice as if he were addressing his congregation, and he asked me if I had read the Koran. So I said yes, at home I have a copy of it in English. The farrier produced his Arabic copy, reverently passing it to the imam who kissed it and said something which made everyone rise and bow and pray. All the villagers' Korans are in Arabic, though they are Kurds and can't themselves read or speak Arabic. Yet their faith is strong and four of the men are *hadjis*, having made the sacred pilgrimage to Mecca.

The farrier was immensely hospitable; after two bowls of *ayran*, a dish of goat's meat, and a soup of hot *ayran* and greens, it was time to shoe Keyif. Fortunately the man's long experience at the job meant that Keyif stayed calm, though we did have to tie a rope to hold his back legs still, and so, for the time being, ended his and my long obsession with his feet.

19   Interrogation in Kars

From Alem to Ani is about twenty kilometres. Ahead of Keyif's pricked ears were hills of baked and burnt rocks, while the cinders made crunching clinky noises beneath his hooves. It was like crossing the remains of a vast furnace.

An army jeep came along but Keyif and I were not very near the road and, if they had seen us, they seemed to take no notice. A special military permit is required by visitors to Ani, because it straddles the Russian border, and I hoped to acquire one when I arrived there.

Ani is special as the capital city of the Armenians' greatest dynasty; Urartu having been the first dynasty, this area was home to the third and most brilliant, led by kings such as Artaxias; they made an outstanding contribution to civilisation though they are little known to the Western world.

The Armenians were the first people to adopt Christianity officially – in AD 301, while Constantinople followed twelve years later. They also pioneered styles of church architecture. Having gained technical mastery of the construction of a central dome, the Armenians used a basic cruciform shape which was apse-buttressed with four main axial buttresses, and usually with four secondary buttresses in the corners. From this the architects began experimenting with variations; using clover-leaf patterns and making a nave with aisles, extending the western barrel vault, or elongating the north and south apses to produce transepts; and by the tenth century they were building hexagonal churches with multi-apsed buttresses. The startling thing about Ani's churches was that no two had the same ground plan.

It was too late to reach there before dark so I stopped at a hamlet for the night. At 3 a.m. there was a thunderous knocking on the door. It was the police and they had come to arrest me. They were polite but firm, they had received orders to take me to their headquarters at Kars. I was in a prohibited area. I explained about the Commandant in Digor suggesting I travel this way, but nevertheless I was taken under arrest with my saddlebags to Kars Police Station, arriving at 4 a.m. for an hour's interrogation. Why was I avoiding the road? Why was I travelling so near the Russian border? Was I particularly interested in Kurds? My letter from the Royal Geographical Society which states that I am non-political and merely studying village customs and rural life cut not a lot of ice, but by a stroke of luck a film I made for the BBC a few years ago had been shown that very week on Turkish television. It helped my interrogators understand why I should be riding through Turkey.

They still made an itemised search of my saddlebags. I wanted to laugh at the way they examined my hammock, bits of spare horse tack and bags of pistachio nuts, cereal and dried figs. The police didn't seem to be taking it too seriously either. But the prison door clanged locked all the same as they left, so I slept on some chairs and felt sure that I would be free in the morning.

But by morning they had changed course. I was accused of having no permit for Ani, nor for horse-riding, nor for book-writing. I pointed out that I had not committed any crime, to which they agreed. When the Chief of Police turned up I had to argue for over an hour to convince him I had not intentionally done anything wrong, and just when I thought I had succeeded he demanded my films for examination and development. Slides cannot be locally developed, so I said he had a choice, he could trust me, or he could spoil my films. It was a long morning, and an even longer afternoon.

Whenever I thought I was free, something else would crop up. At one stage I seemed threatened with deportation. We played some little power games but at all times the police treated me with great courtesy and politeness. Eventually, one of them procured a permit for Keyif and me to be in the prohibited area, and a second permit for me to ride to Ani. Late in the evening my release papers arrived, we all signed them and the police drove me back to the hamlet near Ani. The family were asleep but they awoke and welcomed me with warm smiles, and told me that they had already laid out a mattress and quilt ready for me.

In the morning my host's brother, Ghengis, showed me the track to Ani because he wanted to take a message to his shepherd. On the way I noticed a sledge-cart, built with flat snow-runners instead of wheels. Ghengis explained that sledges are always used in winter when there's about two metres of snow, and they are pulled by oxen or horses.

Ani came into sight on a plain above the gorge of the Arpaçai river. Even from this distance it looked exciting. I could see tall buildings rising from a mass of ruins. The fortress had been built during the fifth century AD, the city was proclaimed capital of the Armenian Bagratid kingdom in about AD 960, and in 1045 it became part of the Byzantine empire though Armenian and Byzantine Christians were always separated by bitter political conflicts. The track went down into a shallow canyon whose sides were honeycombed with Christian cave tombs, man-made in tufa rock similar to the chapels I had seen three months previously in Cappadocia.

By a stream Ghengis met his shepherd, and we also met some soldiers who had come to fill water containers. We were beneath the old city walls, huge blocks with stone crosses carved in them, and decorated lines of stones in herringbone pattern.

At the main Lion Gate, so named from its relief of a running lion, soldiers checked my permit and one escorted me around. The first church we visited was dedicated to St Gregory, built in AD 1215 in typical Armenian style. Now half in ruins, the remaining half bares its interior to the world. Yet its frescoes endure, illustrating the life of St Gregory and the conversion by him of Armenia to Christianity.

The imposing square building I'd seen from the plain was, fittingly, the early eleventh-century Grand Cathedral, minus its dome, designed by Trdat, the same architect who rebuilt the dome of St Sophia in Istanbul. Its altar has ten blind arches; the pillars that once held the dome soar effortlessly upward and the space produces wonderful echoes.

Nearby is a church which was turned into a mosque by the Turks. Only the unusual polygonal minaret and one wall of red stone pillars are still standing, the vaults below have caved in. From here I had a magnificent view of the river gorge. The soldier said we must not point at Russia but he indicated a small square church on an island between a tributary and the Arpaçai. The river was flowing fast and deep, beneath a ruined single-span bridge. There had once been a monastery flanking the bridge, the soldier said, built in 1066. The date jolted me into a completely different historical perspective for a moment.

The prettiest church, to my mind, was a small two-tiered cylinder built in 994 by a king from Horasan. Its lower tier has six circular lobes and the upper layer twelve arches. The final place we stopped had been turned into a mosque, cannibalised from the stones of old churches, complete with scrolly crosses and Seljuk cupola, but it had been transformed back into a church when Ani was recaptured by Christians.

From Ani I rode on across a plain scattered with the remains of churches and monasteries, now just an arch in a cornfield, or pillars and remnants of a fallen dome beside a gulley. The plain is bounded by two lines of mountains, and there used to be fortresses at strategic points along them, for this is a gateway to the Russian steppes. Ahead I noticed a car parked by the roadside with familiar-looking men grouped around it. Kars police. They had come to arrest me again.

They were apologetic about the arrest and took me out to lunch with the *muhtar* of Ani before escorting both Keyif and me back to Kars. Keyif was forced to run the fifty kilometres in four hours of midday heat, by the end he was nearly wrecked, he just stood pitifully with his head hanging low. A policeman took him away to be stabled. I went back into the police station, 'Oh no, not you again!' said the men who had signed my last release papers.

I tried to keep calm and find out the source of the new trouble, but no one could tell me, and they didn't seem to know what to do with me either. So I politely made myself as much of a nuisance as I know how, continually borrowing people's pens to write new statements, asking for tea, and generally getting in the way of everyone's work. Food was brought in for me, bread and honey, it's said that Kars honey is the best in Turkey but it's known to be dangerous if the bees have taken nectar from a certain type of azalea whose honey sends people mad. This was even noted by Xenophon. Mine was delicious but accidentally I dripped some on a file of papers and realised I'd succeeded in being more of a nuisance than I'd meant.

An interpreter took me to the office of the No. 1 chief, a holy of holies where people bow and grovel and speak in hushed tones. I argued and jumped up and down for emphasis. When the interpreter translated my statement I kept butting in to drive the points home. The chief asked him what was my purpose in entering the province through a forbidden back door, and the interpreter replied ruefully, 'She was only looking for a blacksmith.'

The chief lost some of his formality and before long we were amicably drinking tea. Another hurdle had been cleared. But a brick wall lay ahead. I didn't think there could be anyone more important than this No. 1 chief, then I discovered that the Governor of Kars had become involved.

The Governor of Kars was flapping because the Russians had telephoned him on a top security line and reported a horserider in the border zone. The Russians said that I had been under surveillance for two days and they were worried about my purpose. My case had become a matter of national security.

I could not be released until the Governor was satisfied, but he wasn't prepared to listen to my side of things. My escort marched me down to the No. 2 chief's office. He was on the telephone and when the call was over he said that the Governor's office had decided that I must sell my horse immediately.

'No,' I refused flatly. 'There is no law against me owning a horse.' The idea of being forced to sell Keyif brought out a wild stubbornness in me, and I added, 'If the Governor wishes to make a new law saying that a tourist cannot own a horse, let him do so, and I'll take my horse out of his province.'

The No. 2's face fell, he had hoped for an easy conclusion. He telephoned the Governor's office and relayed my refusal. Rapid talk followed, then he hung up and said 'All right, but you've got to go to Erzurum and stop travelling.'

That was another bad idea, like a red rag to a bull and by now I was enraged, 'The Governor may control Kars province but he doesn't have the right to tell me what to do in any other province. I want to speak to the Prime Minister.'

'But the Governor is afraid for your safety, he fears you may fall off your horse and be injured.'

'Tell him that I have survived 10,000 kilometres by horse in far wilder countries than this, he has no cause for alarm.' But the Governor wouldn't listen. Doubtless he was afraid that he would be held responsible for me. We had hit a stalemate.

Neither the Governor nor I would back down, though I was racking my brains to find a way whereby the Governor could appear to have won, yet Keyif and I could go free. So I offered to leave Kars province with my horse by the quickest route. This proved acceptable; I would be given a police escort out of the province. We would leave in the morning.

The No. 2 chief smiled, and he assured me that if in future I should wish to visit Kars I would be most welcome. But if I wanted to do any unconventional things I should write to them asking for permission which they would be pleased to arrange.

I did not have to spend another night in the police station, they offered to pay for me to stay at a hotel. We drove there in a police van and I reflected wryly that, as a tourist, all I'd seen of Kars town was through barred windows and from the back of police vehicles. Not that it wasn't an appropriate way to visit Kars, a frontier garrison town whose atmosphere is grim like a penal colony. Apparently men stationed here all count the days until they can leave.

Many buildings look more Russian than Turkish, which is not surprising since Kars was part of Russia for over forty years until the 1920s. It has a grim history. During the Crimean War the town was occupied by the Turks who resisted a Russian force four times their strength, and held out against a five-month siege, though few were left alive by the end.

I went for a walk, but there was nothing to see, just drab grey houses and dour grey people.

Keyif and I left the province of Kars under police escort and made our way to Erzurum where I was delighted to see Sema again. I didn't unpack, my plan was to leave again next morning and ride north. But Sema had some bad news: 'The police are looking for you.'

Oh dear, that was the last thing I wanted to hear.

'They found out we are friends and came to see me. They said I have to report you to them immediately.'

My instinct was to run away, collect Keyif and vanish from Erzurum, but I couldn't do that to Sema, and since I had kept within the law and played straight up until now, it would be foolish to put myself in the wrong by fleeing.

With a heavy heart I presented myself to Erzurum police station. Lengthy interrogation ensued. I said that I would be selling my horse soon, because we'd had a wonderful journey and he was due for a long rest. Now I wanted to visit Tortum, accessible by road to the north, and would probably return to Erzurum afterwards. I didn't say if I was going by bus or by horse, and they wisely didn't ask.

At the end of it I was given an official letter of clearance. 'Take this with you and if you have any trouble, just show it and you will be released.' I could hardly believe I was free.

It seemed sensible, since my leg was still not right from the dog bite, to check out the danger of rabies. At the hospital I was told that a woman had just died of rabies and I should have begun a long nasty course of injections immediately the dog bit. But that was two weeks ago. Now it was too late. I wasn't anxious, since the numbness didn't hinder my mobility, and I told myself it would doubtless go away of its own accord.

Armed with the letter of clearance and a new map, I packed my saddlebags and rode out of town, heading north along the road for Tortum like a docile tourist. In the final suburbs the vehicle workshops' signboards read 'Oto Elektrik', 'Oto Lastic' and 'Oto Tamer', I wondered if the last was like a Lion Tamer.

We left Erzurum behind and crossed the plain. The odd clicking of Keyif's hooves on the asphalt told me he had two loose shoes. At a village I located a farrier, he had three old nails which he straightened out and hammered into the looser shoe. Even if he'd had more nails he wouldn't have managed to fit them, Keyif was behaving badly again, fresh from his two-day rest. It was embarrassing, me trying to say he was a quiet horse while he lashed out violently whenever anyone tried to pick up his hind feet. He was never this naughty before, and I blamed that young blacksmith who hit him on the nose; now he was afraid of being shod.

Twenty kilometres from Erzurum a gravel track led up into mountains and a man told me it went to a sacred spring. Had I promised to stick to the road? That could be the sacred spring which is famed as the first source of the Euphrates. It was enough to persuade me. The side road followed the course of a stream, babbling and crystal clear, and passing a deeper pool. I spotted some trout. On the bridges there were carpets drying, part of the spring-cleaning for the festival of Bayram which would begin in five days' time and is the most important Islamic celebration of the year. Early evening sun made the lush valley glow, and outlined clumps of hollyhocks with haloes of light. At last I relaxed and felt free of trouble.

We stopped for the night in a village where a wedding had just finished. It surprised me that the bride wore a long white dress, just like a Christian bride. We arrived as the young couple drove away in a battered taxi to spend their honeymoon at an uncle's house in Trabzon.

The village *muhtar* looked after me, and took me visiting.

At one house the owner showed me the pelt of a brown bear he had killed last year. The creature had been as tall as me, and the skin was complete with head and long brown snout. A wolf-pelt was also produced for me to admire, long-bodied and short-legged, black and tan like an elongated alsatian.

Four soldiers arrived from a nearby outpost wanting to buy a ram for Bayram. Every year over 2½ million rams are slaughtered in Turkey at this festival. The *muhtar* produced various sheep for the soldiers to make their selection and they chose the biggest and fattest, costing the equivalent of £20, a typical village price.

The next morning after breakfast Keyif and I climbed a long steep mountain; whenever I thought we had reached the top it would turn out to be only a shoulder hiding a higher pass. Very high up I began hearing the noise of running water.

On a plateau where herds of sheep were roaming, we reached a source in a boggy patch of ground, but I felt sure it wasn't the spring I was looking for. A biting cold wind made me shiver and there was some snow on the northern slopes still in August.

Keyif made good speed across the undulating plateau and at last the sacred spring came into sight, within an old stone wall which marked it as a place of pilgrimage. It was a circular pool made perfectly round and edged by stones, its water bubbling up from the depths, icy cold. I filled my water-bottle, and wondered how long the water from here takes as it slowly becomes the mighty Euphrates in its course through Turkey and Iraq to the Persian Gulf. Then I circled the spring three times, which is the traditional pilgrim's way of making a wish.

Beyond the source the track petered out and the mountain slopes fell away in a series of ravines down to distant lowlands. My map marked a continuing route, so I kept going and decided to ask the way at the next *yaila*. But the only man I could find there was a silly one who giggled at me and said he'd never heard of any of the villages on my map. Eventually he pointed me in entirely the wrong direction.

He went back into his tent and, ignoring his directions, I aimed west over some craggy mountains.

From high points I plotted our course, deciding which slopes were feasible, where to change valleys, and whether the valley bottoms were too rugged for safety. On steep downslopes Keyif kept sliding and slipping, unable to get a grip with his worn-out shoes.

We continued down and as hours passed the valley narrowed until we had to squeeze between rocks and through marshy areas of bushy vegetation. I began to wonder if I had imagined the plain lying beyond.

There were raspberry bushes, blue-thorn shrubs, and wild roses; and where the stream widened into a rock pool I couldn't resist taking a swim. In fact I took several swims as we ambled slowly down that pretty valley and, later in the day when I found a pool and bank of clover hidden from sight, we stopped to camp. It had been rare to find a place where Keyif and I could camp without worries of being disturbed. The night was clear and very starry at this elevation. I slung my hammock between bushes and slept peacefully.

In the light of morning I sat catching up with my diary, having not written for days since I didn't want to be seen making notes after my Kars problems. The only life I saw here was a fox which trotted by unconcerned.

Continuing on our way, I blindly assumed that the path would go where I wanted. Several kilometres later it opened on to foothills above a plain, and a man scything hay told me that we were approaching Erzurum. I thought he just couldn't read my map, but he named all the local villages, and within five minutes' ride I suddenly saw Erzurum lying spread over the plain ahead. Drat. Perhaps the giggling nomad had not directed me the wrong way from the sacred spring after all.

So I tried cutting cross-country to the north-east, foothills became mountains again, and boulder-fields made progress slow but by late afternoon we had reached a high promontory where a shepherd was camped. In reply to my query about an onward route he said he'd shortly be riding to his village on the far side, but first he would make a pot of tea. A welcome idea. We sat outside his tent above the panorama of Erzurum's plain and sipped tea as the sun set. I could even make out Sema's apartment block.

My reverie was broken when Keyif's tether came unknotted and, realising he was free, he ran towards the man's stallion, neighing his war cry. We both leapt up and forced Keyif to swerve. He ran away from us, shaking his head and snorting. Dusk was falling. Recapturing a loose horse can be difficult at the best of times, Keyif was playing games and loving it. Our only hope was the other stallion which he wanted to fight. Keyif kept coming close, and galloping away, infuriating both us and the other stallion. The latter then tore his tethering stake out of the ground and the two horses closed in battle.

Their squeals rent the dusk sky, they reared up and struck out with hooves and teeth. It would have been magnificent to watch but we couldn't be spectators. The shepherd's horse tether came within my grasp so I grabbed it and with a stone hammered the peg back into the ground. In that instant the shepherd caught hold of Keyif's rope, and so we managed to drive the animals apart with no damage done to either horse. But night had fallen and we would have to ride on in the dark.

We saddled our horses and I rode a few paces behind my companion, out of kicking distance yet able to follow in his steps. Sparks flew from the metal shoes of the leading horse when he stumbled on rocks. Keyif was more sure-footed and mountain-wise than he and never tripped. Stars came out one by one but no moon.

Distant oil-lamps in cottage windows marked the village and I found I was guest of a prosperous owner of many sheep, who camped out at his *yaila* for pleasure in the simple life. We ate an excellent supper of corned goat meat and *mast* with freshly-baked bread, and all fifteen of his family came to say hello.

In the morning I looked out on to a garden full of sunflowers, and when we left I chose a route which cut forward towards the Tortum road, reaching it at a place I'd passed three days previously. From a stone shack, which I hadn't noticed before, came the noise of hammering and on the offchance of it being a forge I called out, '*Siz nalband var*?' (Are you a blacksmith?). Our luck was in. The smith was in the process of making ox shoes, crescent-shapes of metal, two for each hoof. He inspected Keyif's hooves and said that he had no shoes to fit but would make some new nails, and it wouldn't take long.

He hammered each bulky red-hot nail-head into a square-ish knob, flattening it into leaves on three sides which he explained would make them wear better. It's odd how the welfare of an animal's feet could seem to dominate my daily life.

I was delighted with Keyif's new stud-headed nails, and the apprentice who had pumped the bellows, and spent five years so far in training, told me his master was the finest farrier in the province. I hoped this was true, but still felt I should warn the man that we'd have to tie up Keyif's hind legs to immobilise him. 'There's no need,' replied the farrier, expertly clipping a twitch on Keyif's nose, and he walked around picking up each

hind hoof without any trouble. The nail-fitting was a great
success, and when it came to paying, the cost was 200 Turkish
lire (20 pence).

20 A sheep for Bayram

At noon next day I rode into Tortum, and tethered Keyif outside a shop while I bought barley. The crowd which gathered were of one voice. 'That's a lovely horse,' and someone offered me two horses in exchange for him. I refused but the offer made me proud of Keyif, because I truly knew that he is far more than just a good-looking horse.

Inevitably later I would have to sell him, but I wasn't prepared to think about that until we had finished travelling in Turkey's north-east corner. Finding a home wouldn't be difficult; in various villages I'd had good offers for him. The only thing worrying me was that if I sold him in a village he could be used to pull a plough, and if I sold him in a town, he would probably have to pull a cart. But I felt sure that the right home would be found, eventually.

Now we rode on, leaving Tortum Valley and heading for the village of Tortumkale up a dry tributary. A dusty sultry day, it was hot being low in the mountains, but rewarding for as we trudged up the stony gorge it opened out until I could see ranges of mountains towering up and outlined against further ranges each a paler shade of blue. Below them in my valley and guarding the entrance to the gorge, was a squat crag crowned by Tortumkale fortress.

I wanted to climb up to the castle, but first I had to find somewhere for Keyif to eat and relax. This led me to the Kirmizi family who sat me in their orchard and fed me hazel nuts and sour cherries, and stabled Keyif beside a young heifer which was due to be slaughtered on the morrow's Bayram.

One daughter, Sevim (whose name means lovably sympathetic), accompanied me to the castle, a short walk and a stiff climb up scree. The lower fortifying wall has crumbled in parts but there remains half of a barrel-vaulted church with alcoves. The upper fortress is perched right on the peak, a tall castle which had once been about four storeys high, but is still awesome. Its walls are nearly two metres thick, and made of rounded rocks held in local mortar, unlike the mammoth stone blocks I had seen in Van's Urartian forts.

Above a long sheer drop stands a square-cornered tower whose walls are badly cracking open, it was sad to think that in a few years the fortress could be gone. Rubble to rubble. Sevim said that her father could remember back to when it was whole and far taller. She led the way down, wearing plastic sandals several sizes too big and hopping on to rocks that slid downhill. That gave me confidence and it was certainly the quickest way down.

Back at the house we relaxed on the upper-storey verandah which looks out at the castle, watching the sky darken and listening to a chorus of bullfrogs. Over supper of stuffed vine-leaves, Sevim's father, Yumus, suggested I stay for Bayram which I accepted with pleasure, and also the girls' offer of a private wash with a bucket of hot water. It made me visualise a bath, a whole bath filled with hot water, but the idea by now seemed very foreign and extravagant.

Early morning found me again sitting on the upper verandah watching Bayram activity as a mob of men came out of the village mosque. No women among them, women have to pray at home. The men made a procession to the graveyard and sat in groups beside the graves of their forebears.

Our breakfast was a special one with soup of *ayran*, rice and spices, savoury pastries and sweet *baklava*. Afterwards, when the family gathered to kill a fat-tailed ram, knives were sharpened and a strange little ceremony took place. While Yumus softly stroked the ram's throat with the knife, all the men joined in a wistful lilting song. The throat was cut, its blood poured into a shallow pit, and each of the children dipped a finger in the blood and put a spot of it on their forehead. They also marked mine.

To skin the ram, Yumus cut a small flap of skin on one hind leg and pushed a stick up its leg to open a hole, and blew into the hole until the corpse had completely inflated. This helps the skin pop loose from the body. Once removed it was salted and folded, while the carcass was butchered into joints and divided among the family. Its fat-tail flaps of solid fat were also shared out as a delicacy. One joint was cut and hammered to tenderise it for immediate cooking. It tasted excellent, and was followed by more honeyed *baklava*.

Mid-morning produced a steady flow of neighbours and relatives to drink tea and shake each other by the hand. Women kissed the man's hand and touched it to their foreheads as a gesture of great respect. All the villagers were dressed in their finest clothes and the atmosphere was like Christmas.

An old woman challenged my right to celebrate Bayram since I was not Moslem, so I explained that the story of Bayram is not only in the Koran, it's also part of the Christian Bible. Bayram celebrates the time when the childless prophet Abraham had prayed for a child, and God sent him a son, Isaac. In return Abraham promised to do whatever God asked, and God told him he must sacrifice his son. The prophet went to do this, telling Isaac why he must die, and Isaac accepted the fate. Just as Abraham was about to kill the boy, a ram came along, and God said 'I tested you and found you worthy, keep your son, and sacrifice this ram.' Part of Abraham's special significance for Turkey comes from his stay in the Haran area of the south-east.

At noon Keyif's stable companion, the young heifer, was slaughtered. The performance was the same as for the ram but without inflating the skin, and the blood was also smeared on the orchard's fruit trees to make them more abundant.

The family would spend the rest of the day quietly, but the late-afternoon sun was so golden that I decided to saddle Keyif and continue our journey. It had been a wonderful day, and for me it had not yet ended.

After a fond farewell we trotted along a dirt road heading west beside a trout river. Both Keyif and I were on top form, he swung along with his head high and I sang songs like 'Land of Hope and Glory' that echoed where cliffs overhung the track. Mountains plunged down to hem in the river's lush green banks. Ten kilometres brought us to the village of Alapinar, the track crossed the river via an old stone bridge and on its parapets sat a row of elders who stared at me in puzzlement.

A decisive young man strode on to the bridge, blocking our path, his presence was larger than his body and he simply took control of the situation. 'You have come to stay at our village, put your horse over here.' I began to protest that I was just passing through but it was useless. 'Now you must come and see our caves, my name is Mehmet and I would like to introduce you to these men.' Then came a string of introductions to kindly smiling people, yes of course I would stay.

The village was a particularly picturesque one of old stone

cottages, with an air of prosperity. In fact most of the villages I'd seen north of Erzurum seemed wealthier than in the south. A horde of urchins materialised as our escort to the five caves high in some cliffs, going up like mountain goats, leaving Mehmet and me scrabbling along in their wake. But they waited for us at the final part of the ascent, a sheer rock face where one had to seek out niches for fingers and toes. It was dizzy-making.

The caves were prehistoric man-made defensive positions out of reach of attackers and wild animals. We crouched in the mouth of the largest cave, looking out much as the original inhabitants must have done.

Dinner that evening was at the *muhtar*'s house, and being Bayram we feasted on mutton and gravy, and *pekmaz*, a mulberry dessert that is reputed to help cure ulcers and stomach ailments. In the morning I strolled around while apricots were being laid out to dry in the sun and some men made a wooden two-wheeled ox-cart. I wanted to take some photographs but the urchins made it impossible, rushing in hordes into every picture, swarming over buildings and being thoroughly silly. This was fairly typical of any village children whenever I brought out my camera.

Keyif had been stabled with chickens, under their roosting pole, so his back was covered in chickenshit. He looked pathetic and I had to laugh. I sobered up when he inadvertently trod on my foot, his new nail-studs were grindingly painful on my toes.

From Alapinar we zigzagged up into mountains, through a haze of purple bluebells, Keyif's springy pace making good speed. The road seemed to vanish but from the top tableland I could see a hamlet about three kilometres ahead, backed by some patches of forest and old snowdrifts. The mountains were rocky with great slabs of stone. We stopped to picnic in the middle of nowhere, then cantered past that village and up into another range of mountains; soon we were higher than anything else in the massive mountain panorama. It was another top of the world.

To the south-east the mountains became sharper and we paused to rest on a headland whose view stretched on three sides into seas of peaks, most of them still below us. It gave me a strange feeling of power. Villages and roads, tracks and paths showed against the short turf, like a map in relief. Our way north led among purple daisies and yellow pompom flowers as tall as Keyif. Crickets chirred and a skylark soared and dived. By the time we reached the valley floor it was sunset and we followed a dirt road by the light of a full moon which turned the scenery into a world of black and white. At the hamlet of Derinpinar, I stayed with the *muhtar*, and dined in a style befitting the second day of Bayram at a relative's cottage. The *muhtar*'s wife and direct family were away at their *yaila*, but at bedtime he laid out a mattress for me on the floor of his own bedroom. He had been *muhtar* for thirty years and was now an old man, so he seemed to think this was perfectly proper.

The next day was one of saddle-shedding steepness. I dismounted to spread the risk, and occasionally I kicked a stone over the edge of the narrow path watching it bounce for hundreds of metres and hoped Keyif would realise he had to concentrate. It worried me that when flies bothered him he would shake his head so roughly it threw him off balance, and here there was no room for even a small sideways step. My thoughts went back to that hairy descent we made from the Van mountains and I realised that we were growing accustomed to using such paths in an everyday way.

At gulleys where rain had washed away the path's ledge, I encouraged Keyif to cross quickly before the ground could collapse. A sudden jerk on the rope and the commotion of scrabbling hooves warned me of trouble and I leapt forward pulling, though it flashed through my mind that my puny weight wasn't enough to stop him falling. The path under his hind hooves had given way, he clawed frantically as the land slid, and somehow he was quick enough to haul himself back on to the path before the fall commenced.

We walked on, up and down, into sheltered alpine meadowland, across a dry riverbed and up again. The next crest brought vistas of misty mountains, and as we moved into the exposed descent, the sky clouded over and began to spit rain. It was a long treacherous descent, so rocky that finally I understood the value of Keyif's closed shoes and gave thanks for them. The stream in the valley was shaded by walnut and willow trees, and had banks of clover where we rested. After fording the stream we joined a dirt road, the shade of trees was a welcome novelty. At a roadside teahouse an old man invited me in for tea and asked where I was going.

'To see the ancient church-mosque of Bağbaşi,' I replied. Bağbaşi village is several kilometres up a side-turning and I reached it just as men were gathering for prayer. Not the best moment to visit a mosque, so I bought barley for Keyif while I had a special 'third day of Bayram' lunch of stuffed tomatoes and *baklava*.

When prayer time was over I rode up to the mosque. It had originally been built in the ninth century as a monastery and chapel to the Mother of God. Later the Moslems had found it so beautiful they restored the main roof and dome. I entered the walled churchyard through an arched stone gateway, a cool mossy place, and could see a gabled chapel with crosses inscribed in its stone bricks. Grass and stunted trees were growing up from its roof. The main church has adjacent chapels, ruined barrel-vaulted chambers with little faced stonework. In the part of the church now used as a mosque the frescoes have of course been removed to keep men's minds on their prayers, and the floor is richly covered in local red patterned carpets. A caretaker arrived and said that it isn't permitted to tether a horse to a mosque, so I apologised and rode away.

My map showed that my next destination, Dikyar, lay about seven kilometres as the crow flies over the mountains, and twenty-two kilometres by road. Someone showed me the start of a footpath, reluctantly and with dire warnings. The path wasn't too terrible and it was stunningly beautiful high in those mountains. From one headland I caught a glimpse of the main road far below us, the vehicles on it looking like children's toy cars.

The scramble down to Dikyar was quite a slide. Suddenly I tripped and went flying off a ledge, my fists clamped to Keyif's leading rope, but he didn't stop, he kept walking and I was dragged along on the end of the rope. Rocks tumbled, Keyif began to get frightened and I prayed he wouldn't bolt away. '*Yavaş*, whoa,' I called, trying to sound calm while I fought for dear life. Though the ground underfoot fell away I managed to pull myself up to a ledge, and took more care after that.

In Dikyar I met a young woman who invited me to her orchard, where Keyif grazed and we ate tiny sweet pears. I offered an apple to Keyif but he didn't know how to bite it open, he had obviously never eaten one before.

We came down to Tortum lake, a beauty spot, then up into its wild hinterlands where almost every village has a ruined church or castle, while others we found simply lost and forgotten in the wilds. At Çamleyamak I visited a tall domed church with a bas relief of the magi carrying gold, frankincense and myrrh, and by the fourth and last day of Bayram I was riding above the tree-line again. I breakfasted sitting on a rock and feeling like an eagle in its eyrie.

As Keyif and I progressed over that range I could see where the mountains plunge onwards to the Çoruh river gorge and its tributaries, of which Tortum river is one. The descent would be long. When we reached the Çoruh we would be among rice paddies and mosquitoes.

Much had already changed as we moved north towards the Black Sea. With the forested land, wood is readily available for building, and villages have gabled two-storey houses with rickety wooden balconies sprouting from whitewashed stone. Grape vines trailed over trellises, from which also hung baskets of drying fruit, buckets and washing. The shops along some village streets reminded me of Wild West movies with their wooden signboards and horse and donkey hitching rails.

In the Çoruh valley we reached the village of Çeltik Kuzu and stayed with a family who were so delightful that I didn't want to move on. So I made a temporary base there from which I roved around visiting the many Georgian churches and castles in the area.

Among the local people I noticed several Laz, recognisable by the shape of their head which usually is flattened at the back with very sloping forehead. Laz are not Turkish, but the indigenous inhabitants of the Black Sea coastline, and their language is close to Georgian.

From Çeltik Kuzu I went to Ishan, which was the most beautiful church I had seen. In the eighth and ninth centuries it had been a Georgian bishopric. Its arches soar still holding the conical roof, designed to raise one's eyes towards God and, looking up into its dome, I could see blue frescoes of the heavenly host. Outside there were trees and a fountain where I picnicked off fresh peaches and dried mulberry syrup, which look like brown plastic, but taste good.

The furthest north-easterly point of my journey was Ardahan, where Turkey bulges into Georgian Russia. The highlands between Şavşat and Ardahan were unlike anything I'd seen before in Turkey, thickly timbered, with alpine meadows and hamlets of dark wooden A-frame buildings as in the Swiss Alps.

Soon it would be autumn; haystacks were mounded to capacity, fruit was being harvested, and people came down from

their *yailas*, closing them for the year. Back in Çeltik Kuzu I
helped the women of the household to slice windfall apples
for drying for the winter. The bruised ones would be dried
separately as extra cattle fodder.

It was a long job. Every now and then a woman would join
in until she had to go off on other chores. Whenever the heap
grew small, someone would upturn another sack of windfalls
on to the wooden terrace. The women told me that in ten years'
time the dam across the Çoruh at Yusufeli would be completed
and all their valley would become a lake. Çeltik Kuzu would
exist only as disintegrating stonework underwater.

One evening a forest ranger rode into the village, to the house
where I was staying. He had heard about Keyif and wanted to
buy him from me. I said no, unable to bear the thought that it
was time for Keyif and me to part. But it *was* time, we had now
finished our journey and Keyif deserved a long fattening rest.
After saying no I almost regretted it, because the ranger
wouldn't make Keyif pull a cart. His job was to ride around the
forests checking that no one was stealing trees. Keyif would
enjoy that, and with the local abundance of barley and apples,
this would be a good place for a horse to live.

The ranger came back the following evening on his own
horse, when I was with Keyif by the village fountain. Keyif
heard the hoofbeats and neighed his lusty roar that made other
horses sound tinny. The man asked again about buying Keyif,
offering to sell his horse and borrow the rest of the money. In
the end I agreed. His horse looked well-fed and obviously
well-tended but was old. Keyif couldn't have found a better
home.

A day later we concluded the sale. I insisted on keeping
Keyif's beaded bridle. While the men wrote out the note of sale
I said goodbye to Keyif. He was no longer my horse. Then I
watched him be led out of my life. Without him there was
nothing else I wanted to do, and I packed my bags to leave.

The next morning the family loaded my baggage on to a
mule, the girls put flowers in my hair, sat me on top of the
wooden pack saddle, and escorted me out down to the river.
To ride a mule, after Keyif's swift paces, seemed a joke.

The village receded into the mountains. At the dirt road
alongside the Çoruh River we flagged down a *dolmuş*, the
girls kissed my hands and cheeks in fond farewell, and I said
goodbye to one of the happiest episodes of my life.

After the *dolmuş* ride I caught a bus to Erzurum. Through the windows I kept catching glimpses of the mountains Keyif and I had crossed, things I'd seen before from high above, distant villages we'd been to, the village where the blacksmith straightened three old nails, the mountains where we'd got lost. I sat silently watching it unroll, and could hear that people on the bus already knew my story; men from Tortum and Yusufeli were telling people how far Keyif and I had travelled, and when someone asked if I'd had a good horse, the men replied vehemently, yes, a very beautiful one.

It made my heart ache. Not with sorrow. With happiness.